The Best
Stage Scenes
of 1994

edited by Jocelyn A. Beard

The Scene Study Series

SK
A Smith and Kraus Book

Published by Smith and Kraus, Inc.
One Main Street, Lyme, NH 03768

First Edition: January 1995
10 9 8 7 6 5 4 3 2 1

The Scene Study Series ISSN 1067-353

NOTE: These scenes are intended to be used for audition and class study; permission is not required to use the material for those purposes. However, if there is a paid performance of any of the scenes included in this book, please refer to the permission acknowledgment pages to locate the source who can grant permission for public performance.

Contents

Scenes for Women

Scenes for Men

Preface

1994 was a great year for fantasy. An ancient yet hip Indian god follows the exploits of two women from suburbia in Terrence McNally's A PERFECT GANESH, an unhappy ghost stalks the stage in Nicky Silver's PTERODACTYLS, two paranoid men inadvertently chase one another to THE ENDS OF THE EARTH in a play by Morris Panych, and Robert Coles continues his saga in the irrepressible CUTE BOYS IN THEIR UNDERPANTS FIGHT THE EVIL TROLLS. From the very light to the extremely dark, many of the plays of 1994 found themselves taking off into the strange ionosphere of their playwright's imagination, making for some very startling theatre. Ghost characters are regaining their popularity, which is wonderful, for who is more free than a ghost to express her/himself? After all: where would Mr. Shakespeare be without unhappy spirits with big mouths?

1994 was a great year for realism. The tragedy of World War II is relived in Diane Samuel's haunting KINDERTRANSPORT while the heroism of those who fought is honored in THE GATE OF HEAVEN by Lane Nishikawa and Victor Talmadge. David Hare takes the British judicial system to task in MURMURING JUDGES while Daniel Magee shows us the other side of the coin in the bone-chilling PADDYWACK. Back on this side of the Atlantic, the plight of slaves is told in elegant prose by Rita Dove in THE DARKER FACE OF THE EARTH, while a different kind of American experience was chronicled in Robert

Schenkkan's ambitious THE KENTUCKY CYCLE.

From the ridiculous to the sublime, 1994 was a nicely appointed season. The representative scenes in this book will provide you, the performer, with a wealth of fresh new material to work with. I have made every effort to select scenes with well-drawn characters, clearly defined dynamics and exciting dialogue, and with plays by the likes of Tom Stoppard, Michael Frayn, Cheryl L. West, and Martin Crimp to choose from this has been a most enjoyable task! Don't you wish you had my job?

Break a leg!

—*Jocelyn A. Beard*
Patterson, NY
Autumn 1994

I would like to dedicate this book to Melette, who was spelled wrong last time.

Introduction

Here's a collection of scenes that provides a collage of distinct voices, styles and ideas from some of the best new writers in the English speaking theater. Included are excerpts from plays by such luminaries as Tom Stoppard, Brian Friel and Terrence McNally, as well as scenes by many writers whose work will be new to all but a few theatrical insiders. Most of the selections are by American writers, but there are also a few scenes from exciting new Canadian, Irish and British writers whose work is just beginning to receive the notice of American theater artists.

While the collection is a rich source of material for actors, it also works as a sample of contemporary play writing, useful to theater professionals and enthusiasts who want a taste of the work of emerging playwrights. After reading through the scenes, I promptly ordered the plays of several writers whose work was unfamiliar to me.

For actors, there are many good choices of material to work on without you or your teacher being influenced by famous productions or star performances. These are pieces that you can feel free to develop, experiment on and make *yours*. Take your time selecting a piece. Some of the scenes are realistic, some are more theatrical and some are deliciously weird. Find a scene that genuinely appeals to you. "Try on" several of the scenes by reading them with your partner as part of the selection process. Once you commit to one, find and read the whole play to give your-self a context for what happens in the scene. It also helps to read other plays or stories by the same author to get a sense of their unique voice and style.

If you're working without a director to shape and interpret the scene, here's two cents worth of advice to get started. The one thing *all* of the scenes have in common is that at least one of the characters makes a discovery or realization during the scene. That moment of discovery is the *event* that you and your partner are dramatizing. All the choices that are available to you, char-acter, movement and props, should contribute clearly and com-pellingly to illuminate this event. Decide with your partner where the most important moment of realization happens. What are the series of steps that make it happen? Remember that act-ing is a team sport. Are you providing the appropriate and spe-cific counter-force that your partner needs? These choices can be "roughed in" by discussing and reading through the scene, but you'll make the real discoveries by fully committing to running the scene as many times as you can.

Above all, enjoy the work and the process of rehearsing the piece. Acting class is a place where the joy of creating and learn-ing should take precedent over everything else. Good luck!

—*Joseph Hanreddy*
Artistic Director
Milwaukee Repertory Theater

The Best
Stage Scenes
# of 1994

The Best
Women's and Men's Scenes
# of 1994

ARCADIA
Tom Stoppard

1 Man, 1 Woman
Septimus Hodge (22) tutor of Thomasina Coverly (13) a precocious young girl.

Scene: A large country house in Derbyshire, 1809

News of an affair between Mrs. Chater (the wife of a visiting poet) and a mysterious man has reached Thomasina via the butler. When Thomasina grills Septimus on the details of human love as it physically manifests itself, he has no choice but to respond to her questions truthfully.

O   O   O

THOMASINA: Septimus, what is carnal embrace?

SEPTIMUS: Carnal embrace is the practice of throwing one's arms around a side of beef.

THOMASINA: Is that all?

SEPTIMUS: No... a shoulder of mutton, a haunch of venison well hugged, an embrace of grouse... *caro, carnis;* feminine; flesh.

THOMASINA: Is it a sin?

SEPTIMUS: Not necessarily, my lady, but when carnal embrace is sinful it is a sin of the flesh, QED. We had *caro* in our Gallic Wars —"The Britons live on milk and meat"—"*lacte et carne vivunt.*" I am sorry that the seed fell on stony ground.

THOMASINA: That was the sin of Onan, wasn't it, Septimus?

SEPTIMUS: Yes. He was giving his brother's wife a Latin lesson and she was hardly the wiser after it than before. I thought you were finding a proof for Fermat's last theorem.

THOMASINA: It is very difficult, Septimus. You will have to show me how.

SEPTIMUS: If I knew how, there would be no need to ask *you*. Fermat's last theorem has kept people busy for a hundred and fifty years, and I hoped it would keep *you* busy long enough for me to read Mr. Chater's poem in praise of love with only the distraction of its own absurdities.

THOMASINA: Our Mr. Chater has written a poem?

SEPTIMUS: He believes he has written a poem, yes. I can see that there might be more carnality in your algebra than in Mr. Chater's "Couch of Eros."

THOMASINA: Oh, it was not my algebra. I heard Jellaby telling cook that Mrs. Chater was discovered in carnal embrace in the gazebo.

SEPTIMUS: *(Pause.)* Really? With whom, did Jellaby happen to say? *(Thomasina considers this with a puzzled frown.)*

THOMASINA: What do you mean, with whom?

SEPTIMUS: With what? Exactly so. The idea is absurd. Where did this story come from?

THOMASINA: Mr. Noakes.

SEPTIMUS: Mr. Noakes!

THOMASINA: Papa's landskip architect. He was taking bearings in the garden when he saw—through his spyglass—Mrs. Chater in the gazebo in carnal embrace.

SEPTIMUS: And do you mean to tell me that Mr. Noakes told the butler?

THOMASINA: No. Mr. Noakes told Mr. Chater. *Jellaby* was told by the groom, who overheard Mr. Noakes telling Mr. Chater, in the stable yard.

SEPTIMUS: Mr. Chater being engaged in closing the stable door.

THOMASINA: What do you mean, Septimus?

SEPTIMUS: So, thus far, the only people who know about this are Mr. Noakes the landskip architect, the groom, the butler, the cook and, of course, Mrs. Chater's husband, the poet.

THOMASINA: And Arthur who was cleaning the silver, and the boot-boy. And now you.

SEPTIMUS: Of course. What else did he say?

THOMASINA: Mr. Noakes?

SEPTIMUS: No, not Mr. Noakes. Jellaby. You heard Jellaby telling the cook.

THOMASINA: Cook hushed him almost as soon as he started. Jellaby did not see that I was being allowed to finish yesterday's upstairs' rabbit pie before I came to my lesson. I think you have not been candid with me, Septimus. A gazebo is not, after all, a meat larder.

SEPTIMUS: I never said my definition was complete.

THOMASINA: Is carnal embrace kissing?

SEPTIMUS: Yes.

THOMASINA: And throwing one's arms around Mrs. Chater?

SEPTIMUS: Yes. Now, Fermat's last theorem—

THOMASINA: I thought as much. I hope you are ashamed.

SEPTIMUS: I, my lady?

THOMASINA: If *you* do not teach me the true meaning of things, who will?

SEPTIMUS: Ah. Yes, I am ashamed. Carnal embrace is sexual congress, which is the insertion of the male genital organ into the female genital organ for purposes of procreation and pleasure. Fermat's last theorem, by contrast, asserts that when x, y and z are whole numbers each raised to a power of n, the sum of the first two can never equal the third when n is greater than 2. (*Pause.*)

THOMASINA: Eurghhh!

SEPTIMUS: Nevertheless, that is the theorem.

THOMASINA: It is disgusting and incomprehensible. Now when I am grown to practice it myself I shall never do so without thinking of you.

SEPTIMUS: Thank you very much, my lady. Was Mrs. Chater down this morning?

THOMASINA: No. Tell me more about sexual congress.

SEPTIMUS: There is nothing more to be said about sexual congress.

THOMASINA: Is it the same as love?

SEPTIMUS: Oh no, it is much nicer than that.

ARTHUR AND LEILA

Cherylene Lee

1 Man, 1 Woman

Leila (50s) a Chinese American woman, and Arthur (60s) her alcoholic brother

Scene: Los Angeles

Arthur has been selling little bits of junk to Leila, claiming they are valuable family heirlooms. Here, Arthur arrives—uninvited—at her home, and the unfortunate animosity between the siblings becomes more than apparent.

O   O   O

(*Arthur comes to Leila's house. She is in the kitchen cooking. She doesn't notice her brother until he speaks, startling her.*)

ARTHUR: Surprise! Your favorite brother!

LEILA: Arthur! Omigod, was the door unlocked? Anyone could have wandered in. What are you doing here?

ARTHUR: I came to visit my little sister. Aren't you glad to see me?

LEILA: You have to leave.

ARTHUR: (*Looking around.*) Your kitchen faces North. Not auspicious. Bad Fung Sui. I hope the toilet faces East. What would mama say if your toilet didn't face East.

LEILA: I'm very busy, Arthur. I'm having my board members over. My help is sick, there's no one to come in at the last minute, I'm cooking—

ARTHUR: What are you cooking?

LEILA: A soufflé. I'm sorry, but you have to leave. Things have to be quiet around here. I don't want my soufflé to fall.

ARTHUR: I like that.

Leila: No, you can't stay, I'm not inviting you. Please try to leave quietly. My soufflé.

ARTHUR: Like the kitchen god listening for gossip.

LEILA: What?

ARTHUR: Thousand year old eggs, pei don. The women roll them in sawdust, bury them in the yard, and then must keep silent for twelve weeks. No gossiping or the kitchen god hears and the eggs won't be preserved. I always liked pei don.

LEILA: That's not for pei don. That was for hom don, salty eggs, and the silence was only for six weeks.

ARTHUR: Never liked them as much.

LEILA: You have to go, I have a million things to do.

ARTHUR: I could help. What do you need? Someone to serve drinks? Or maybe taste your concoctions, like the emperor's food tasters, make sure nothing is poisoned.

LEILA: I don't need your help. I need you to leave. (*Leila pushes up her sleeves as she gets back to cooking.*)

ARTHUR: Where is your jade bracelet, Leila? The one mama gave to you.

LEILA: I'm cooking. I don't wear it when I'm cooking. It could get damaged.

ARTHUR: You take it off? Aren't you afraid you might lose it?

LEILA: I'm very careful with my things.

ARTHUR: I know. You place great value on them. Appearance is so important.

LEILA: And yours is uninvited.

ARTHUR: You should be wearing your jade bracelet. A mother's gift to protect her daughter. The bracelet accepts the impact before misfortune hits, didn't mama teach you that? A good daughter wouldn't take it off. You should always wear it so the jade grows—

LEILA: Grows greener from my body heat. I know, now please—

ARTHUR: Such a valuable gift. A mother puts it on her daughter's wrist to prevent injury, break the fall. It's your protection. What would mama say if she knew you weren't wearing it? Very bad luck to take it off.

LEILA: I don't have time to discuss this, Arthur, please go away.

ARTHUR: I brought you something, Leila.

LEILA: Such a shame you can't stay—

ARTHUR: It's a button. A very important button. It's very old, over one hundred years. Made of pearl. I think mama kept it because it reminded her of her mother. Paw paw used to make frogs, Chinese buttons, remember?

LEILA: Let me see. (*She takes the button.*) This isn't pearl, it's plastic.

ARTHUR: You said you wanted something beautiful. See by that greasy spot? There's a nick where mama's needle caught. How many times did she sew this on? Isn't that beautiful? You think about that.

LEILA: Please go. This isn't the time or place for business. You're supposed to call, you know the arrangement.

ARTHUR: Two men came to visit me the other day. They are interested in Chinese antiques. Lofon. They drove a white Mercedes. I don't know how, but they knew about papa's old store. They kept encouraging me. I told them to come again.

LEILA: We made an agreement. You aren't to sell to anyone else. Everything belongs in the family. You promised.

ARTHUR: Shh. Your soufflé. We just talked. Talk is cheap, Leila, you know that.

LEILA: Talk with you has never been cheap.

ARTHUR: Maybe I'll let them look.

LEILA: Look!

ARTHUR: To evaluate, appraise.

LEILA: You don't even let me look. I'm your sister.

ARTHUR: Shh. Your soufflé.

LEILA: Don't let them look. They shouldn't be allowed. I don't pay you for that.

ARTHUR: I know. Such a lovely home, I always wanted to have a look inside. (*He moves to get past her.*)

LEILA: (*Blocking him.*) No strangers. Who knows what they will do? Having them fingering mama's undergarments. (*She shivers.*)

ARTHUR: It isn't up to you, Leila. Papa left everything to me. His firstborn male heir, the one he sent back to China to learn the old traditions. Those Lofon men were very impressed with my knowledge of Chinese classics. They wanted to know if I might have relics from the ancient Chin Dynasty. I told them it was possible, it is the family name.

LEILA: Don't be absurd. (*Beat.*) Arthur, there was a Chinese plate. One with different scenes painted on it. Each scene had all these people in it, depicting battles, the emperor's court. But there was one panel where there were only two people in it. Two women. I remember because it's the only one that wasn't crowded with faces. I used to count the faces. That's how I learned my numbers. In the panel with only two women, there were trees painted, flowers, a branch with two songbirds. One woman was dressing the other or maybe she was giving her something. It was next to papa's herb cabinet. I would like to have that plate. I would pay a lot to have it. Do you remember it?

ARTHUR: (*Nodding as if almost remembering.*) No. I think you are mistaken. Chinese scenes always have three people in them, to make sure there are no secrets.

LEILA: I remember it well.

ARTHUR: The memory can play tricks. Perhaps some of your "fund-raising" would help me to remember. Know what I mean?

LEILA: Can't you see I'm in the middle of cooking? I don't have money on me.

ARTHUR: I could give you a discount, Leila, for buying...sight unseen. Best to buy quick. Bargains don't last. Lofon interest in old things always doubles the price.

LEILA: Don't you dare do business with those men. Don't let them look. You have to show me first.

ARTHUR: Shh. Your soufflé, Leila. Shouldn't you check it? (*Leila turns away to check her soufflé. It is in trouble.*)

LEILA: Oh no! Now what am I going to do? Arthur, this is all your fault, you had to barge in—GET OUT! (*Arthur makes a hasty exit. Leila turns back to the disaster, rubs her bare wrist.*) My protection. (*Lights fade.*)

BEFORE IT HITS HOME

Cheryl L. West

1 Man, 1 Woman
Wendal (40s) a jazz musician dying of AIDS, and Reba (50–60)
his mother.

Scene: Here and Now

Wendal has returned to his parents' home where he hopes to be able
to fight his disease. Here, he breaks the tragic news of his condition to
his mother with unexpected results.

o   o   o

REBA: *(Looks up at Wendal who's still standing away from the
table.)* Wendal?

WENDAL: *(Looks at all of them for a moment, hesitates.)* Sorry
Mama. I think I lost my appetite. *(Wendal exits. Lights. Later on
that night. Wendal comes downstairs. He's sick. With much effort, he moves to the kitchen and gets ice water from the refrig-
erator. Takes his medicine, moves back to the living room. Reba
enters wearing a robe. Wendal quickly hides the medicine.)*

REBA: I didn't know anyone was down here. You feeling any better?

WENDAL: A little.

REBA: How 'bout some ginger ale? I don't know why, I just woke
up and had a taste for some pop. You want some?

WENDAL: No.

REBA: Sorry everything didn't work out like you planned this
evening. *(Pause.)* Everything was going fine. Why'd you have to
fight with him?

WENDAL: *(Moving to the couch.)* Why don't you ask him that question?

REBA: *(Walking around the room.)* I'm glad you and Junior gon'
paint in here. I'm a help. Since you all been here I feel kinda

useful again. Lately, I seem to have a lot of time on my hands. Sometimes I catch myself sitting all day right there on that couch and Lord this house can get so quiet. With Dwayne not needing me as much... don't get me wrong, I'm not complaining. He's got a mind of his own, just like you did. Scares your father. Sometimes a father can't see his son for his own failings. You ever think about that?

WENDAL: Oh Mama. Why do you always defend him?

REBA: *(As if she didn't hear him.)* Oh me and Maybelle go but sometimes I think about what if... what if something happened to your father... he never wanted me to work. I ain't never been nothing but somebody's mother. And today I wondered if I had even been good at that. *(Wendal looks at her directly and she at him.)* I defend him for the same reason I defend you... because you both a part of me. Now why don't you tell Mama what's bothering you. I let it go for a week but something's eating you alive, I saw it when you first walked through that door.

WENDAL: Nothing.

REBA: *(Firmly.)* I asked you a question. Don't let me have to ask you twice.

WENDAL: I haven't been well Mama. Been a little under the weather.

REBA: *(Relieved.)* Well, we'll just have to get you better. It's probably one of them flu bugs going around...

WENDAL: It's not that simple.

REBA: I'll make an appointment the first thing in the morning with Dr. Miller and...

WENDAL: Has he ever treated an AIDS patient?

REBA: *(Not registering.)* Oh, he's treated all kinds of things. *(What he said sinking in.)* A what?

WENDAL: I have AIDS Mama.

REBA: Well we'll just get you there and have him check you out.

WENDAL: Mama, do you ever hear what people really say? Did you hear me say I have AIDS?

REBA: No Wendal. AIDS, I don't know nothing about it. You ain't got that.

WENDAL: I do.

REBA: What I just say? I don't know nothing about no…

WENDAL: I'm sorry.

REBA: Oh my God tell me you kidding Wendal.

WENDAL: I wish.

REBA: Bailey…

WENDAL: I haven't figured out how to tell him.

REBA: How? How did you get something like this?

WENDAL: I don't know.

REBA: *(Her anger and fear out of control, loud.)* What do you mean you don't know? You come home and you're dying of some disease and you don't know how the hell you got it.

WENDAL: I'm not dying. I have…

REBA: Did you have some kind of surgery and they gave you bad blood?

WENDAL: No. What difference does it make how I got it?

REBA: You been lying to us. You been home here and you ain't said a word…

WENDAL: Every day I tried to tell you… I practiced this speech…

REBA: I don't want to hear no damn speech. I want to hear how the hell you got this? You're not one of them… that why you got so mad at dinner?

WENDAL: Mama.

REBA: No. No. I know you're not. You've been living with Simone…

WENDAL: *(Carefully choosing his words.)* Mama, you know that I never was quite right like Daddy used to say… *(No response from Reba.)* Try to understand Mama. I have relationships with women and sometimes with men.

REBA: No you don't, un-un. No you don't. You're my son, just like Junior …you're a man. You're supposed to…

WENDAL: Supposed to what? Be like Daddy. His world don't stretch no farther than this couch…

REBA: Boy, who the hell are you to judge anybody?

WENDAL: Mama, it's not much different than you and Auntie May.

REBA: What you say?

WENDAL: It's not so different than how you feel about Auntie May…

REBA: How dare you? How dare you twist me and Maybelle's relationship into this sickness you talking. That woman is like a sister to me. You hear me? A sister!

WENDAL: A sister that might as well live here. You closer to her than you are to Daddy.

REBA: *(Enraged.)* You shut up. Shut your mouth. Shut your filthy mouth. Don't be trying to compare that shit... my life ain't the one on trial here.

WENDAL: I'm sorry. I just thought you might understand Mama.

REBA: UNDERSTAND! How can a mother understand that? How can I understand that you're one of them people, that I raised a liar for a son... I was so happy...

WENDAL: Mama, forgive me. I would've done anything to spare you...

REBA: Is that why you don't come home?

WENDAL: It's hard pretending.

REBA: You don't have to pretend with us. We're your parents...

WENDAL: Yeah, right. Dad can't stand to hear anything about my life and where does he get off having Dwayne call him Daddy?

REBA: *(His last words lost on her.)* Couldn't you have given us a chance? Maybe we would have...

WENDAL: *(Softly, tries to touch her.)* I am now Mama.

REBA: *(Shudders at his touch, sharply.)* Don't you tell your father. You hear me? I'll tell him. It'll kill him if it came from you. *(More to herself.)* I should've never let you leave here. Bailey told me... said I kept you too close, wasn't no room left over for him... he told me no good would ever come to you... he told me... *(Yelling.)* You better get down on your knees right now boy and you better pray, beg God's forgiveness for your nasty wicked ways...

THE CAVALCADERS

Billy Roche

1 Man, 1 Woman
Terry (40s) a man incapable of letting go of the past, and Nuala (20s) an emotionally unstable young woman.

Scene: Ireland

Nuala and Terry have been having an affair for some time now, and Nuala's passion is starting to border on the psychotic. Here, the two argue over Terry's estranged wife, providing him with the perfect opportunity to end things.

O   O   O

NUALA: You've cut yourself again.

TERRY: What?

NUALA: You've cut yourself. Why don't yeh wear the gloves I gave yeh.

TERRY: I do sometimes.

NUALA: I wish yeh would. *(She kisses his hand.)* I really wish yeh would… What are yeh thinkin' about?

TERRY: Nothin'.

NUALA: Yeh never talk to me, Terry. Yeh never tell me anythin'.

TERRY: I tell yeh all yeh need to know.

NUALA: Yeah but yeh don't say the things I need to hear though, do yeh? I'm crazy about you, yeh know. You're the love of my life. I mean it. I love yeh Terry…Did yeh hear what I said to yeh? *(Terry sighs, rises and begins to dress.)* Yeh treat me so cruel sometimes, Terry. Yeh really do.

TERRY: Jesus Nuala, stop will yeh, and don't start.

NUALA: What's that supposed to mean?

TERRY: What's it supposed to mean? In all the time that you've been comin' over here did yeh ever once hear me say that word?

NUALA: What word?

TERRY: You know what word.

NUALA: Love?

TERRY: Yeah. Did yeh ever hear me say it? *(She shakes her head.)* Did yeh ever hear me mention it—or hint it even? Yeh didn't, did yeh? *(She shakes her head.)* Right. I mean to say you can say it all yeh want. It's your prerogative. Maybe it makes yeh feel good or somethin'. I don't know. Or maybe you need to find justification for all this. But I don't, yeh see.

NUALA: I say it because it's true.

TERRY: No. You say it because yeh want to hear the words reverberatin' back to yeh. You think you're up in the Alps or somewhere. Well you're not in the Alps. You're in the lowlands lows girl—the same as meself!

NUALA: If I thought you didn't love me I swear I think I'd…

TERRY: What?

NUALA: I don't know. I'd throw meself off of the bridge or somethin'.

TERRY: Now do yeh hear that… Do yeh know somethin', I ought to give yeh a backhander for that, that's what I should do. I mean look at yeh. Hangdog! You're twenty-two years of age for Jaysus sake! I'm nearly twice your age and I feel younger than you do.

NUALA: I've given yeh so much, Terry. I've given yeh everythin'. I've poured out my soul to yeh and I hardly know anythin' about you.

TERRY: Well what exactly is it yeh need to know?

NUALA: I don't know.

TERRY: What?

NUALA: I need to know what she looks like.

TERRY: What?

NUALA: Your wife?

TERRY: What about her?

NUALA: I've been told that yeh still carry a photo of her with yeh in your wallet everywhere yeh go.

TERRY: Who told yeh that?

NUALA: Is it true?

TERRY: What if it is?

NUALA: I want to know what she looks like.

TERRY: Why?

NUALA: Because I just need to know that's all.

TERRY: Oh yeh just need to know! Jesus… God, give me patience!

NUALA: I found out where she lives, yeh know… I found out where she lives and I went to her house to see her.

TERRY: When?

NUALA: One day last week.

TERRY: How did yeh get up there?

NUALA: Took a train.

TERRY: Are you mad or what?

NUALA: Don't say that to me Terry… It's all right, yeh needn't worry, I didn't go near her or anything. I just hung around outside the house for a few hours that's all.

TERRY: Yeh didn't see her? *(Nuala shakes her head sulkily.)* Nobody home?

NUALA: Some fella on a walkin' stick… But I need to know what she looks like though Terry, yeh know. I mean I really need to know what I'm up against.

TERRY: Oh yeh need to know what you're up against! That's different. Why didn't yeh say so. I mean if yeh need to know what you're up against! Well I mean…

NUALA: What?

TERRY: Hah?… Jesus! *(He paces about irritably.)* Right! Alright. Here. *(Angrily he takes out a photo and forces it upon her.)* Here. There. Now. Now yeh know. Are yeh happy now? Hah? Yeah? Happy? …Now do you think for one minute that you can compete against that. Do you seriously think for one minute that you can compete…

NUALA: That picture's nearly twenty years old. She don't look like that any more.

TERRY: That's not what I asked yeh. Do yeh think you can compete against it, is what I'm askin' yeh.

NUALA: Yeah I do.

TERRY: How?

NUALA: Easy.

TERRY: How easy?

NUALA: What?

TERRY: How easy, I said. Hah? *(Nuala, in a fit of rage, snatches the photograph from his hand and tears it in two, throwing it on the floor. Terry takes her by the hair and slings her to the ground. He bends to pick up the pieces.)* Don't you ever touch anythin' belongin' to me again.

NUALA: She don't look like that now.

TERRY: You're fuckin' neurotic, yeh know. A fuckin' fruit cake yeh are.

NUALA: Well at least I'm not walkin' around in someone else's shadow all the time, anyway.

TERRY: What's that supposed to mean?

NUALA: He took her away from you and now you're takin' it out on me. But I'm not the one who needs to be forgiven...

TERRY: Do yeh know somethin', all those head shrinkers you're goin' to are beginnin' to take effect on yeh, I think.

NUALA: Because I'm not the one who hurt yeh. I didn't do yeh any wrong Terry...

TERRY: But if you're goin' to start analyzin' anybody then I'd prefer if yeh picked up somebody else, if yeh don't mind. Preferably somewhere else...

NUALA: Maybe yeh need to forgive yourself for callin' him a friend in the first place.

TERRY: You don't know nothin' about it.

NUALA: I know... I know...

TERRY: What do yeh know? What is it yeh know?

NUALA: I know that he was supposed to be your best friend and he let yeh down—stole away your wife from yeh, moved in with her above the little baker's shop right across the street from there.

TERRY: Ain't that awful what I've to listen to, too...

NUALA: And it used to break your heart to have to stand here and look at the two of them goin' in and out every day, holdin' hands and talkin' and laughin' and lookin' at one another and all…

TERRY: Two weeks in a funny farm and she thinks she's a professor or somethin'.

NUALA: But he didn't give a toss about you—not a toss. Of course you thought the sun, moon and stars shone out of him. Rogan could do no wrong as far as you were concerned. Rogan did this and Rogan did that and Rogan did the other thing and everybody knows he never did nothin' really. While you were walkin' the slippery pole and swimmin' the river or runnin' races he was standin' there like a duke in blue jeans by Jaysus lookin' at himself in a shop window. A real little shit goin' around if yeh ask me. Couldn't even get his own girl!

TERRY: Oh, you'd know of course.

NUALA: But unfortunately he's not goin' to bring her back to yeh Terry. I'm sorry to have to be the one to inform yeh and all but…

TERRY: The day I need a headbanger like you to tell me how to live my life…

NUALA: She's not comin' back to yeh Terry.

TERRY: Is the day I'll lie down and…

NUALA: She's not comin' back boy. Yeh may forget about her. She's not comin' back.

TERRY: I know she's not comin' back.

NUALA: Well what are yeh waitin' for then? Hah? What are yeh waitin' for?

TERRY: If you think now for one minute that I'm goin' to stand here and listen to you bullshittin'…

NUALA: What are yeh waitin' for?

TERRY: What am I waitin' for? I'll tell yeh what I'm waitin' for. Do yeh want to know what I'm waitin' for? I'm waitin' for you to get the f… *(Red with rage, hands clenched Terry looks around for something to vent his spleen on. Nuala watches him calmly. When his rage has passed he stands breathless, holding on to the counter. Nuala moves towards him with tender eyes.)*

NUALA: I'm the other half of you, Terry, you're the other half of me! *(Terry sighs, chuckling through his exasperation.)*

TERRY: I don't think you should come over here any more, Nuala.

NUALA: What?

TERRY: I'm no good for yeh… I'm only usin' yeh, sure!

NUALA: Usin' me? What do yeh mean—"usin' me"?

TERRY: What are yeh wantin' me to do, spell it out for yeh or some-thin'? …Don't look at me like that. It gives me the creeps when yeh look at me like that. I mean to say that's the very thing now that… Look I'm old and you're young. You need somebody young—someone who'll talk to yeh and all, tell yeh things. You need help! Yeh should be able to see through fellas like me anyway. I mean to say, Jesus Christ, I'm practically whatdoyou-callit…

NUALA: What do yeh mean, "usin' me"?

TERRY: Usin' yeh, usin' yeh! I'm only usin' yeh! *(Terry looks into her fawnlike eyes.)* Look Nuala. Look. *(She breaks away.)*

NUALA: I'm a person, Terry. There's a person inside of me.

TERRY: I know you're a person. If I didn't think there was—a person inside of yeh, I wouldn't be tellin yeh' not to come over here any more now, would I? Hah? Now would I?

NUALA: If I thought I'd never see you again I think I'd die.

TERRY: Yeh won't die at all.

NUALA: I would. Give us a chance, Terry. I'll do anythin'.

TERRY: There's no point, Nuala. We've already done everything worth talkin' about and it just don't seem to make any differ-ence. I mean I just don't really feel anythin' for anybody any-more yeh know. I mean… Ah I don't know… Look, just take your things will yeh and go. Go on and don't come over here again.

NUALA: What? *(Terry turns away from her.)* I have things to offer, Terry. I mean I'm worthy of… I mean… I'm a worthy person… I mean Breda says that he was only a little shit too, yeh know—couldn't even get his own girl!

TERRY: Breda! *(He sniggers softly.)*

NUALA: I know you're really a nice fella at heart, Terry. I know yeh are.

TERRY: I'm not. At heart, or on the surface, or any other way, I'm not a nice fella. I'm not!

NUALA: What?

TERRY: Believe me Nuala, I'm not!

NUALA: I could help yeh to forget about her though Terry, yeh know.

TERRY: What?

NUALA: I said I could help yeh to forget about her.

TERRY: Go ahead home Nuala, will yeh. Go on, get out of here. And stay away from here altogether in the future.

NUALA: You don't really mean that Terry.

TERRY: What?

NUALA: You don't mean that.

TERRY: What is wrong with you eh? I mean where's your pride? Don't you have any pride? I'm tryin' to dump yeh here, and here you are standin' there like an ejit takin' it all. I mean where's your pride, girl? Hah? Hah? I mean, Jesus! ...Hello, is there anybody in there? Hah?

NUALA: Why are yeh doin' this, Terry?

TERRY: Look, just get out of my life, will yeh. Go on, beat it...

NUALA: What?

TERRY: What? What? What? Yeh should see yourself there. You're like a fuckin' puppet on a string or somethin'. The big bulgin' eyes on yeh! So? What?

NUALA: What? To tell yeh the truth Terry, I'm half afraid to go. I mean if I go...

TERRY: If yeh go, yeh go. So go!

NUALA: What? Where?

TERRY: What do I care. I mean I don't care where yeh go, do I. Just go. Back to your Da's farm or somewhere. Back to the funny farm if yeh like. I mean I don't care. It makes no odds to me one way or another where you go or don't go, because you don't mean doodle shit to me like, yeh know. I mean I swear I don't give you one second thought from one end of the day to the next. Yeh know? Doodle shit! That's all you are to me.

NUALA: What?

TERRY: (Mimics her.) What? (Nuala suddenly grabs her things and ~tearfully, banging the door behind her. Terry stares toward ~way. He sighs. Pause.) God forgive me.

COUP DE GRACE

Bill Ohanesian

1 Man, 1 Woman
Donald (30-40) the recently deceased husband of Marla (30-40) the grieving widow.

Scene: A mortuary room

Donald has committed suicide in order to spite Marla and their highly volatile relationship. Here, Marla vents her anger and grief over Donald's dead body, and they both discover that not even death can put an end to their foolish bickering.

O   O   O

DONALD: Umbrellas up, dear colleagues! For upon the far horizon blows…
(As a female mourner enters, draped in funerary black, a veil covering her weeping face. This is Marla, Donald's widow. Slowly, deliberately, she steps up to the casket.)
DONALD: …the weepiest of widows, come to drench us all in her tidal wave of tears.
MARLA: Donald, it's me. I'm here to say… good-bye.
DONALD: —Good-bye! Next! *(Silence, as Marla struggles for words.)* Come, come. We are all waiting…
MARLA: I… don't know how to say everything… I need to…
DONALD: *(With a yawn.)* I have no doubt you will anyway.
MARLA: What's my problem? I'm just talking to myself…
DONALD: My dear—perhaps what you need is a SIGN. *(As he raises his hand up from inside and snaps several times right in her face. But of course, she doesn't react. Marla tries several times to speak, then,)*
MARLA: It's just…that there's so much we never allowed closure to.
DONALD: "Allowed closure to?" How new age. Or in your case— old hat.

MARLA: *(A long silence, then,)* I know. It was because of me. After sixteen years together, I failed you. Forgive me, Donald… it's all my fault.

DONALD: Well! After sixteen years of discord, despair and bad coffee, we finally achieve a rare and wholehearted agreement. — OF COURSE it's your fault!

MARLA: Then again, I suppose I'll never know. How could I? You didn't even leave a note… or a letter…*(—At which, Donald sits up in his coffin for the first time, wearing a devious smile. He stares at the grieving Marla, then,)*

DONALD: So you noticed… my piece de resistance. My coup de grace.

MARLA: But I tried, Donald. For sixteen years I tried to find out what you wanted from me… from us.

DONALD: Yes, my dear. —Yet whenever I tried to elucidate your murky despair—

MARLA: And all I got back was your pointless, endless, babbling.

DONALD: I do not babble! I elucidate. Until now. When I depart in perfect, shattering… silence.

MARLA: Until now. When you leave without even saying good-bye. *(As she gathers herself to leave.)* If that's all I meant to you, then it was over a long time ago. Good-bye, Donald. *(Irked, Donald hops out of the casket, hot on her heels.)*

DONALD: No, it's not over! Not when you, as usual, twist things around. Overexaggerate. Overreact. *(When Marla suddenly stops and fires back a final,)*

MARLA: I know I wasn't the perfect wife. But at least I loved you enough to never give up on us like you did. —You… chicken-shit!

DONALD: *(Caught off guard, sputters for a comeback.)* "Chicken-shit?" How erudite! But I am afraid I did NOT—

MARLA: *(Striding to the box.)* You chickenshit son-of-a-bitch!

DONALD: —I did NOT give up on us. I gave up on your distress and despair and—

MARLA: After all I put into this marriage! All those nights I waited up…

DONALD: *(Mocking her.)* …and suffered and grieved and—

MARLA: How could you do this to me? To US? *(As Marla begins pounding on the top of the casket with her fists!)*

DONALD: Marlie! Are you crazy—somebody might— *(But the full force of Marlie's rage is unstoppable. Donald watches helplessly, dodging her blows.)*

MARLA: GodDAMN you!

DONALD: *(With a nervous glance upward, loudly Whispers:)* Marlie, SHHHH! "He" swears as much as anyone, except for THAT word—

MARLA: Goddamn you to rot in hell!

DONALD: *(Trying to cover her mouth.)* I WILL, if you don't shut up! *(Finally, she SLAMS the lid shut and collapses in exhaustion. Donald stand over and gazes down on her for a few silent moments, then;)* That's it? That's all the soul-wrenching grief I merit? *(As Marla catches her breath, it's impossible to tell whether she's absorbing what Donald's saying or utterly oblivious.)* Darling… purge thy guilt! Vent thy rage! Wallow in despair! For meanwhile, I will be bounding through eternity like a gazelle! Gorging upon the fruits of Eden! Defiling virgin maidens from Bali to Barbados! From Kuala Lampur to—

MARLA: *(Suddenly—and as if to herself:)* …New Zealand …Easter Island …Bali. All those places I wanted us to see together…

DONALD: And all of which were quite inaccessible on a teacher's salary. But now, I am quite able to…

MARLA: I think now would be a good time. But… I couldn't possibly afford it…

DONALD: Quite correct. Now—

MARLA: —Unless… I can sell your coin collection… *(At which, a panic-stricken Donald spins her around to face him—though she is oblivious to his actions.)*

DONALD: Are you crazy? Marlie, in seven years, it'll be worth triple—

MARLA: —And that old wreck of yours has been taking up good garage space for years…

DONALD: That "old wreck" as you put it, is a '67 Alfa Romeo! A certified CLASSIC.

MARLA: …and if I can't dump all those Bob Dylan albums on some antique dealer, they're going in the trash.

DONALD: Marla, Marla! Those are memories! Don't you remember… our song…? *(As he begins whistling the melody to Dylan's "I'll Be Your Baby Tonight," then sings:)*
"Close your eyes, close the door…
you don't have to worry anymore…
I'll be your baby tonight…"
(A memory-tender smile warms Marla's face as she closes her eyes and softly sings along as they waltz through the room.)

DONALD AND MARLA: *(In unison.)* "Shut the light, shut the shade…
you don't have to be afraid…
I'll be your baby tonight…"

DONALD: *(By himself, bellows.)* "Well, that mockingbird's a-gonna sail away—" *(Then stops, baffled, as—Marla unexpectedly pulls away.)*

DONALD: *(Trying to rekindle the moment.)* "That Mockinbird's a-gonna sail away…"

MARLA: Oh, Donald, why were we so stupid? Why did we waste so much time fighting instead of listening to each other?

DONALD: I… What about that time in the closet? I listened plenty then!

MARLA: *(Suddenly breaks out laughing.)*

DONALD: And what the devil do you regard so laughable?

MARLA: I don't know why I just thought of it, but… remember that time I locked you in the closet? When you were screaming your head off? Remember? *(At that, "Bridge Over Troubled Water" FADES UP LOUD as they both yell over it.)*

DONALD: *(Covering his ears at the memory.)* Do I remember? Do I remember the full-blast bludgeoning my ears suffered by that Goddamned— (—*Then, reacting to God's WHACK on his head.)* —Ow! All right, I'm sorry. I'm sorry! *(Continues, back to Marla.)* —from that, that… vile Simon and his odious Garfunkel? —And not just once, and not just twice, but over and over and over and over and…

MARLA: *(Laughs heartily at the recollection.)*

DONALD: Now I know why your favorite movie was "Clockwork Orange!" But why so MANY times?

MARLA: I blasted the whole "Bridge Over Troubled Water" album almost five times! You know why?

DONALD: Yes! Because you're a sadist!

MARLA: *(A rush of giggles, remembering.)*

DONALD: I stand corrected. You're a masochist!

MARLA: *(More giggles, then,)*

DONALD: Because you're crazy!

MARLA: Because it took me that long to knock off a whole bottle of Chardonnay! *(And laughs out a real belly-laugh.)*

DONALD: You mean, while I was being brutalized by Mighty Joe Simon and Godzilla Garfunkel, you were getting...

MARLA: —Drunk off my ass! And when I finally let you out? You remember? You were so...

DONALD: *(Mock anger.)* —Mad! Only to find YOU...

MARLA: ...Horny as a hog! *(as they both laugh at the erotic memory, Donald moves close, caressing, kissing her. The music fades down as Marla is overwhelmed by the nearness of Donald's prexence.)*

MARLA: Oh, Donald... *(Realizing she can "feel" him.)* Donald...?

DONALD: Marlie, it's me! It is me!

MARLA: I swear it's like you were right here... *(Unnerved, yet enraptured.)* Is it really you?

DONALD: Yes, I am here! Marla, you can hear me!

MARLA: Yes! Oh, Donald...

DONALD: Marla, why didn't we do the things we really wanted to... like travelling... seeing the world... or even... staying home and... *(With real difficulty.)* ...having children?

MARLA: Instead of putting ourselves through so much hell?

DONALD: Marla, listen—we can erase all our mistakes! Hear me, we can!

THE DARKER FACE OF THE EARTH

Rita Dove

1 Man, 1 Woman
Augustus (20s) an educated slave committed to freeing his people,
and Phebe (20s) a young woman who is fascinated by him.

Scene: A plantation in antebellum South Carolina

On her way back from paying a visit to the local conjuring woman,
Phebe encounters Augustus and the two fall into conversation. The
powerful young man tells her of his near-death experience leading
Phebe to confess her own fear of the future.

O   O   O

AUGUSTUS: Evening.

PHEBE: Evening. *(Tries to walk past.)*

AUGUSTUS: What's your hurry? Why don't you keep me company
  for a spell? Unless you're scared of me, too.

PHEBE: Scared of you? Why should I be scared of you?

AUGUSTUS: *(Smiling.)* I can't think of a reason in the world. Come
  on, rest yourself. *(Phebe approaches slowly, sits down beside
  him carefully.)* Sure is a fine night *(Phebe nods.)* Are you back
  from the shout?

PHEBE: No.

AUGUSTUS: I didn't think you were the sort who went in for that.
  (Scream in the distance.) Poor souls! *(Looks at Phebe.)* You're
  trembling.

PHEBE: I am?

AUGUSTUS: Yes, you are. And I don't believe it's entirely my doing.
  Fear eats out the heart, you know. *(Looking off.)* Fear: how suddenly it can turn! It can topple the strong as well as the weak. It
  can make senators and field niggers alike crawl in their own
  piss. Listen! *(Gesturing in the direction of the "Shout.")* God-

fearing folk. White-fearing niggers. Death-fearing slaves.

PHEBE: Ain't you scared sometimes?

AUGUSTUS: Of what? White folks? They're more afraid of me. Pain? Every whipping's got to come to an end. Now tell me—what could be worse than walking in chains while others dance?

PHEBE: I heard you've been whipped so many times they lost count.

AUGUSTUS: They thought they could beat me to my senses. But when they looked into my eyes and saw I wasn't afraid, they didn't know what else to do.

PHEBE: It'd be something, not to be afraid.

AUGUSTUS: You have to have a purpose. I have a score to settle and I can't die until it's done.

PHEBE: And nobody ever tried to kill you?

AUGUSTUS: Oh, yes. First time, I was a newborn babe. *(Bitter laugh.)* I was hardly alive.

PHEBE: They whipped you when you was a baby?

AUGUSTUS: Daddy was my massa: the night I was born they took me from my mother, put me in a basket, and galloped away. By the time they stopped to take me out my side was torn open. I didn't walk until I was three. So you see, I met death before I was properly introduced to life.

PHEBE: Lord have mercy.

AUGUSTUS: *(Sharply.)* Mercy had nothing to do with it. They threw me out like trash.

PHEBE: But a bastard child's still a slave, and a slave has value. Miss Amalia never seemed to care about Massa's bastard children running around.

AUGUSTUS: *(Lost in thought.)* I believe Death and I have made a pact. He didn't get me the first time, so this time he'll wait till I'm ready. And I won't be ready until I find the man who tried to kill me—my father. Then I will kill him. *(Musing.)* That's how it is: those bounty hunters and overseers can't do a thing to me. Do you know what they see when they look into my eyes? They see Death, smiling out.

PHEBE: Oh!

AUGUSTUS: You've stopped shaking. Now why don't you tell me

what made you that way in the first place?

PHEBE: I can't—

AUGUSTUS: Conjuration, I imagine? Mumble-jumble from that old woman.

PHEBE: Her name's Scylla.

AUGUSTUS: Women like her, huh! They get a chill one morning, hear an owl or two, and snap!—they've received their "powers"! Then they collect a few old bones, dry some herbs, and they're in business.

PHEBE: She told me to watch my footsteps—

AUGUSTUS: —or you'd fall lame.

PHEBE: And to keep my mouth shut when the wind blowed—

AUGUSTUS: —or else the wind spirit would steal your soul.

PHEBE: *(Afraid.)* How'd you know?

AUGUSTUS: You think she's the only conjurer in the world? Why, your Scylla's a baby compared to the voodoo chiefs in the islands. They can kill you with a puff of smoke from their pipe! If you believe in them, that is. Look at me: I carry enough curses on my head to bring a whole ship down around me, but no ship I sailed on ever sank. So if this conjuration is supposed to work, they must be saving me for something special. *(Phebe looks at Augustus with wonder as the lights slowly dim.)*

THE ENDS OF THE EARTH

Morris Panych

1 Man, 1 Woman
Frank (40s) a paranoid man running from someone he fears is following him, and Willy (40-60) a woman with conceptual problems.

Scene: A hotel on an island at the ends of the earth

Frank has traveled to the ends of the earth to escape Walker, a mysterious man he fears means him ill. Here, Frank is served tea by Willy, who seems to be the proprietress of the hotel at the ends of the earth.

WILLY: *(With tea things tottering on tray.)* Here we are!
FRANK: Let me give you a hand with that.
WILLY: Why don't you give me a hand with this?
FRANK: What? No. I was going to give you a hand with that. *(Somehow he's in her way.)*
WILLY: Just sit down. Sit down. I'll do it myself.
FRANK: For heaven's sake. *(He sits down. The chair collapses on one side!)* Ah!
WILLY: Oh. Look at that.
FRANK: That's fine, I'm—fine. *(Sighs.)* Thank you.
WILLY: Why, it's right there in front of you, Mr. Travers.
FRANK: What is?
WILLY: Cream. And sugar.
FRANK: I said "Thank you."
WILLY: You're welcome.
FRANK: *(Ever-so-politely.)* Are you deaf by any chance?
WILLY: Just a little ahead of myself. Let it steep, first.
FRANK: Steep?
WILLY: Oh. Just wait. I'll see what I can find.
FRANK: What? *(Willy goes off. We see blind Alice in the shadows with an ax. She says nothing.)*

FRANK: Oh, good grief. Is there nobody else around here—with whom—one can—communicate—or is that simply too much to ask? *(Alice disappears again, as Willy reappears with an armful of tea towels and a tablecloth.)*

WILLY: This is all the linen there is, I'm afraid.

FRANK: Oh. Thank you. *(She hands the linen to him.)*

WILLY: No one's done any washing of any kind.

FRANK: Yes, well. Perhaps just put them down.

WILLY: Take them. Take them. Why not? It's every man for himself. *(Frank takes them. Willy sits. A moment passes. She smiles.)* What?

FRANK: What? *(Pause.)* Why did you say "What"?

WILLY: *(Looking into the teapot with a flashlight.)* We all have to help each other around here.

FRANK: Really?

WILLY: No. Not quite. Another minute. *(Offering.)* Biscuit?

FRANK: *(Trying to reach.)* Perhaps if I put these down.

WILLY: Yes. Take those. Why not?

FRANK: *(Taking biscuit.)* Never mind. Thank you. *(Looking.)* Oh, dear.

WILLY: It's all right.

FRANK: These are bouillon cubes.

WILLY: Take two.

FRANK: Thank you. One'll be… Mmm.

WILLY: Oh, just slightly.

FRANK: I thought so.

WILLY: And you?

FRANK: Not completely. But I'm getting there.

WILLY: Oh. Well, give me your cup then.

FRANK: Thank you. *(Willy pours, but nothing comes out.)*

WILLY: You like it strong, I hope.

FRANK: A little stronger than that, actually.

WILLY: Sugar?

FRANK: Uh, I think this is cornstarch.

WILLY: Oh, dear. Well, I hope someone gets some more.

FRANK: I said "I think this is cornstarch"!

WILLY: Ha. Ha. Really? And what did *you* say?

FRANK: I said, *"I—think—this—is—corn—starch."*

WILLY: Oh. *(Pause.)* I don't get it.

FRANK: Neither do I.

WILLY: It's been such a long time since anyone else was here.

FRANK: Even longer than that, I imagine.

WILLY: I suppose you'd like to see a room.

FRANK: What? Now?

WILLY: Oh. Well, all right. *(She rises. Suddenly, a knock on the ceiling. Dead silence, and then ever-so-quietly.)* Oh. It's Alice. She's not very fond of visitors, as you can see. *(Rising, Willy heads for the stairs.)*

FRANK: *(Following.)* Alice? Is she someone I should—? Alice? Does she run this place? Is this registering with you at all?

WILLY: I'm beginning to wonder, myself.

FRANK: Yes.

WILLY: *(Stops, out of wind, confused.)* Soap. What about the soap?

FRANK: ...can I give you a hand up the stairs, or something?

WILLY: Perhaps you could give me a hand here? (*Willy heads down.)*

FRANK: Do other people find you as confusing as I do?

WILLY: Do they?

FRANK: Which way are you going?

WILLY: Oh, that's all right then. You go on up ahead. But be careful. We're a few steps short of a stairway.

FRANK: Yes. I'd say so.

THE FAMILY OF MANN

Theresa Rebeck

1 Man, 1 Woman
Belinda and Ren (20–30) two new writers on a highly rated television sitcom.

Scene: Los Angeles

Belinda and Ren have become attracted to one another. Here, they take a rest from the high-pressure world of TV writing and enjoy one another's company.

○   ○   ○

(Ren and Belinda are in bed. He is reading a script. She is going through catalogues.)

BELINDA: You hear the one about the megalomaniac baseball team?

REN: No.

BELINDA: Norman Lear has first base, Jim Brooks has second, Cosby third, and Ed has the whole outfield. *(Ren smiles, scribbling.)*

REN: Come on, he's not that bad.

BELINDA: You know what he told me about that stupid movie he made, I saw that thing, it's the worst movie ever, right? Am I right?

REN: It's not *Citizen Kane*. Okay. It's the worst movie ever.

BELINDA: Exactly. He told me, it was his autobiography. The thing is an adaptation of somebody else's *book,* this other guy wrote the book, and Ed is running around telling everybody it's his autobiography.

REN: He was being metaphoric.

BELINDA: Ed is incapable of being metaphoric. I mean, with all due respect, the guy's a fruitcake, and you're just defending him because he's decided you're his "son." The fact that you grew up in somebody else's house notwithstanding.

REN: Hey. If Ed's decided I'm his son, who am I to say I'm not?

BELINDA: Oh, it's all bullshit anyway. And if I hear one more word about how decent it all is, I may truly puke.

REN: What is the matter with you all of a sudden? What happened to television being like a campfire and you're the great story-teller?

BELINDA: Oh, come on—

REN: No, you come on. You watch a rerun of *The Odd Couple* some night. That show was a thing of beauty. Tony Randall's commitment and, and timing and *pathos*—

BELINDA: Pathos?

REN: Yeah, pathos, you don't see that—I mean, I've read Molière—

BELINDA: Molière? How did Molière—

REN: Yeah, big surprise, the dumb jock reads Molière.

BELINDA: I didn't say—

REN: And frankly, I don't see the difference.

BELINDA: The difference? Between Tony Randall and Molière?

REN: Yeah, that's right. What's so fucking different, Miss Ph.D. in English? You tell me what's so different.

BELINDA: (*Overlap*) Could we not bring my Ph.D. into this, I'm not—

REN: Just answer the question.

BELINDA: You want me to tell you the diference between Tony Randall and Molière.

REN: That's right. Why is fucking Molière so much better than Tony Randall?

BELINDA: I don't know, he just is.

REN: He just is, that's a real compelling argument—

BELINDA: All right. The sophistication of his language, his profound understanding and compassion for human nature even while he's satirizing social—

REN: He's telling the same stories we are. Who gets the girl. Fathers and sons competing with each other—

BELINDA: Oh, come on, Ren, theatre and television are completely different experiences. The theatre is much more—vivid, it's more *humane*—

REN: Yeah, I have seen some class A shit in the theatre.

BELINDA: Of course, but—

REN: In fact, most of what passes for theatre is class A shit. The only people who write for the theatre these days are people who can't get work in television.

BELINDA: Oh, is that so?

REN: And I've read your fucking *New Yorker,* too. Boy, that's good writing.

BELINDA: Ren!

REN: What?

BELINDA: What's the matter?

REN: Nothing. *(Pause.)* I just, I think there's been some great television, and I'd like to write some. Someday. I mean, we're telling stories, right? You're the one who made me feel like this. When you talk about it, sometimes, you make it sound like something holy.

BELINDA: Well, I'm full of shit.

REN: No, you're not.

BELINDA: Yes, I am. Christ, we spend all this time, as a group, going over and over these damn scripts—who *ever* decided that writing was a group activity, that's what I want to know. And you know what else I want to know? Why, if we're going to do ten drafts of a script, it doesn't get better! Why not just shoot the first bad draft? Why shoot the *tenth?* Why do Steve and Sally get to fuck up my work? Why does Ed? I mean, all of this—it isn't about storytelling. It's not even about product. It's just about power.

REN: Then why are you doing it?

BELINDA: *(Pause.)* For the money. *(Pause.)* I mean, I've never had money. I know, you think it's chicken feed, but this is more money than I've ever *dreamed* of, this is—. That's the thing about selling your soul. No one tells you how much they'll actually pay you for it.

REN: You're not selling your soul. I can't believe you. I'd kill to be able to write like you, and all you do is run it down. Nevermind. *(He goes back to the script. She watches him, uncertain, a little embarrassed.)*

BELINDA: I'm sorry.

REN: You don't have to be sorry. I'm sorry. I'm sorry you don't enjoy this more.

BELINDA: *(Making up.)* I'm starting to enjoy it. I'm starting to enjoy it a lot.

REN: Well, you should. Ed is crazy about you. And you love him. Whether you want to admit it or not.

BELINDA: I never said I didn't like Ed. I think he's a nut, and I'm also desperate for his approval. It's an ongoing topic of discussion between me and my therapist.

REN: Well, stop worrying about it. You know, he's bumping up your next episode. He called me yesterday, raving about it.

BELINDA: *(Pause. Positively glowing.)* He did? He liked my script?

REN: He loved it. He loves you. He loves the way you fight—

BELINDA: Forget Ed. What do you like?

REN: I don't like anything at all. *(They kiss.)* Okay. That's all you get.

BELINDA: Come on…

REN: I'm working! *(Giggling, she falls back, watches him for a moment, then looks through her catalogues.)*

BELINDA: *(Musing.)* Hey, Ren? What did you do when you first started making money? I mean, was there a moment when all of a sudden, you had money? You didn't have any, and then you just, had a lot?

REN: Yeah, sure.

BELINDA: What did you do?

REN: I don't know, I… I bought, uh, a box of chocolates. You know, like, a five-pound box of See's chocolates, and I… Fed Exed it to my grandmother.

BELINDA: You sent your grandma chocolates? That's so—

REN: Yeah, okay—

BELINDA: It's adorable!

REN: So what did you do?

BELINDA: I bought sheets. I realized I've been sleeping on the same sheets since college; they're always so expensive, I could never justify buying new ones. So I bought these pretty sheets, with colors, and… I'm sorry, I'm embarassed now. After that spectacular grandma story, I sound so—

REN: No, you don't.

BELINDA: It's just so weird, actually having it. I don't quite know how to spend it.

REN: Tell you what. This weekend, we'll go to San Francisco, rent a suite at the Ritz, and never leave. Order up room service for two days.

BELINDA: Oh, yeah? What will we be doing for two days?

REN: We will be watching basketball on TV. *(She laughs.)*

BELINDA: You are so mean.

REN: Basketball is a beautiful thing.

BELINDA: So how come you quit? I mean, you were a big college star, right? Why didn't you keep going?

REN: Because I was awful. I was the worst basketball player, ever.

BELINDA: But you were in all those big games, weren't you?

REN: Yeah, "big games." That's the NC double A to you, babe. I didn't really play in those games. The coach basically kept me on the team because he liked me.

BELINDA: I don't believe you. Ed says you're great.

REN: Compared to Ed, I am. He is old and weak, and I am young and hard.

BELINDA: *(Laughing.)* Ed's no good?

REN: Terrible.

BELINDA: How's Bill?

REN: Sucks.

BELINDA: Wait a minute. If you guys all stink, maybe I could play with you.

REN: No.

BELINDA: *(Baiting him.)* Why not?

REN: *(Beat.)* You're not tall enough. *(He kisses her as she laughs. Blackout.)*

HELLCAB

Will Kern

1 Man, 1 Woman

Cab Driver (30s) a road-weary novice, and a Lawyer (30s) a woman on her way to the train station.

Scene: A taxi cab

When the Cab Driver discovers that his passenger is a Lawyer, he can't resist an opportunity to express his opinion of the legal process.

O   O   O

(A woman in her mid-thirties gets in. She is a Lawyer and looks it, dressed in a sharp business suit and carrying a briefcase.)

CAB DRIVER: Good morning.

LAWYER: Northwestern Train Station, please. *(The Cab Driver hits the meter, pulls away.)*

CAB DRIVER: You got it.

LAWYER: Got awful cold this morning, didn't it?

CAB DRIVER: Yeah. And the weather guy said snow possibly.

LAWYER: Well, what's a Christmas without snow.

CAB DRIVER: Exactly. So. How you been?

LAWYER: Oh, fine, I guess. I still have a lot of shopping to do.

CAB DRIVER: Time's running out.

LAWYER: I know.

CAB DRIVER: So, what do you do?

LAWYER: I'm a lawyer.

CAB DRIVER: *(Unable to hide his disappointment.)* Oh. Really.

LAWYER: You got something against lawyers?

CAB DRIVER: Well, sure. Doesn't everybody? I mean, let's face it, when it comes to your profession... Well, never mind.

LAWYER: What?

CAB DRIVER: No, forget it.

LAWYER: No, I want to hear this. What is it about lawyers you don't particularly like?

CAB DRIVER: The fact that they're all sharks.

LAWYER: Why do you say that? Do you know any lawyers?

CAB DRIVER: You ever seen a TV show called Court TV? It's got its own cable network station where all they show 24 hours a day is current trials. Mostly sensational stuff. You ought to see the lawyers on that show, boy. Make your hair curl.

LAWYER: Well, if you're talking about the criminal lawyer—

CAB DRIVER: Yeah yeah yeah. Criminal lawyers.

LAWYER: It's pretty well known the worst lawyers are the criminal lawyers.

CAB DRIVER: Get out of here.

LAWYER: No, I'm serious. They become criminal attorneys because they're not smart enough to do anything else.

CAB DRIVER: They teach you that at law school?

LAWYER: It's common knowledge in the profession.

CAB DRIVER: What, are you trying to pull my chain here?

LAWYER: No.

CAB DRIVER: I may be a taxi driver but I'm not stupid.

LAWYER: I didn't say you were.

CAB DRIVER: Well, you can't just make a gross generalization like all criminal attorneys are not as smart as the rest of the profession. I didn't just fall off the cabbage truck, you know.

LAWYER: Now hold on a second. I wasn't insinuating that you had.

CAB DRIVER: You tell me what other profession has public humiliation as an integral part of its system.

LAWYER: And how is that?

CAB DRIVER: You're a woman. You ever seen a lawyer get a woman who claims she's been raped up on the witness stand, asking her how many men she's slept with, and how many times, and going into every detail. It's disgusting.

LAWYER: You can't do that anymore. They've passed laws against that kind of cross examination.

CAB DRIVER: That's just it. It was so rampant they had to pass a law just to keep a lawyer's integrity in check.

LAWYER: But that goes back to the criminal attorneys. The criminal attorneys do that.

CAB DRIVER: I take it all back. Lawyers aren't sharks. *(Pause.)* That's too high up the evolutionary chain. Lawyers are cockroaches.

LAWYER: You can let me out on the corner.

CAB DRIVER: Before or after the light?

LAWYER: Before.

CAB DRIVER: Okay. *(He pulls over and hits the meter.)* $4.00. I hope I didn't offend you.

LAWYER: Oh, no.

CAB DRIVER: We could continue this discussion over dinner if you like. *(The Lawyer laughs, throws money on the seat, and gets out of the cab.)* Hey, I'm a real stud. *(Blackout.)*

HERE

Michael Frayn

1 Man, 1 Woman
Phil (20s) and Cath (20s) a young couple just starting out in life.

Scene: Here and Now

Cath and Phil have moved in together into a tiny room in a boarding house. Close quarters inevitably leads to frayed tempers, and here they argue as only a young couple can argue.

(The bathroom door opens, and Cath appears.)

CATH: ...I can't hear you when I've got the door shut! And don't say leave the door open, because I *can't* leave the door open, because if I leave the door open there isn't room to be in there! *(She goes back into the bathroom.)*

PHIL: I'm not saying leave the door open...

CATH: *(Off.)* And don't say Then don't be in there!

PHIL: I'm not saying Don't be in there...

CATH: *(Off.)* Because I've *got* to be in here if I'm going to have a bath...!

PHIL: I'm not saying anything. *(He picks up the mask and retires to the alcove. He draws the curtain back. It reveals Eric's chair, with books and papers on a small table. He switches on a readinglamp and sits down.)*

CATH: *(Off.)* Oh, really? Well, I'm not listening...! Wasting your breath...La la la la la la la... *(He pulls the curtains closed. She comes out of the bathroom.)* Oh. Though why you're taking refuge in there I don't know, since I'm not in here, I'm in *there!* *(She goes back into the bathroom. He looks out from behind the curtain.)*

PHIL: Why don't you leave the door *half-open?* *(The taps are turned off. She comes out of the bathroom, amazed.)*

CATH: Half-open?

PHIL: Half-open. Yes! Wedge it half-open!

CATH: *Half-open?*

PHIL: Half hyphen open. *(Pause.)*

CATH: Half-open...

PHIL: Half-open. *(He closes the curtain again. She remains where she is.)*

CATH: I suppose all this is really... well...

PHIL: *(Pause. He opens the curtain.)* Really about what?

CATH: You know.

PHIL: No?

CATH: Yes, you do.

PHIL: I haven't the slightest idea what you're talking about.

CATH: I thought I wasn't supposed to say the word?

PHIL: What word?

CATH: Theodore. *(Pause. He closes the curtain.)* Yes, well, I don't know how we can talk about it if I can't say the name. What's wrong with the name? I don't understand! Theodore... Anyway, *you're* the one who put him in there!

PHIL: *(Opens the curtain.)* *I* put him in here? *I* didn't put him in here.

CATH: You did! *(He comes out of the alcove, pulls the toy dog out from some piece of furniture, and whacks it down on to the table.)*

PHIL: *We* put it in there.

CATH: Oh. Yes. Well...

PHIL: You're always doing this.

CATH: Always doing what?

PHIL: Always saying *I* put things somewhere.

CATH: Well, you *did* put this particular thing somewhere!

PHIL: No, I didn't. *We* did. *(Pause.)* We *did!* We *did!* You're always pretending it's me that makes the decisions.

CATH: Because it *is* you that makes the decisions.

PHIL: It's us that make the decisions. *(Pause.)*

CATH: You said We've rather outgrown this kind of thing, haven't we?

PHIL: And you said Yes, we have.

CATH: No, I said If you want to put it in the thing, then put it in the thing.

PHIL: Exactly. So then it's me that decided! That's exactly what I'm saying!

CATH: That what you decided?

PHIL: That you decided I decided!

CATH: What?

PHIL: Look. I said, Do we want to put this thing in the thing?

CATH: No, *I* said, Do *you* want it in the thing?

PHIL: Would you mind letting me finish?

CATH: Go on.

PHIL: Thank you.

CATH: It was exactly the same with the other thing. *(Pause.)*

PHIL: Am I finishing what I'm saying or aren't I?

CATH: Go on, then.

PHIL: I don't mind waiting while you bring up some other subject first. I just want to know which I'm doing.

CATH: Yes. No. Fine. Get on with it.

PHIL: I'm finishing what I'm saying?

CATH: Yes! Finish what you're saying! *(Pause.)*

PHIL: What do you mean, it was exactly the same with the other thing? What other thing?

CATH: Never mind. Go on.

PHIL: If you mean the bicycle…

CATH: No, please. Let's not get back to the bicycle.

PHIL: It wasn't me that brought it up.

CATH: What do you mean, it wasn't you that brought it up?

PHIL: I mean it wasn't me that brought it up!

CATH: Last Saturday! *(Pause.)*

PHIL: *Upstairs.*

CATH: Upstairs, yes!

PHIL: Not up in the conversation.

CATH: What?

PHIL: I didn't bring it up in the conversation.

CATH: In the conversation? No, you brought it up in a towering rage.

PHIL: Anyway…

CATH: Anyway… *(Pause.)*

PHIL: *Our* bicycle, incidentally.

CATH: I *said* "our bicycle"!

PHIL: You said "your bicycle."

CATH: In fact I said "the bicycle."

PHIL: You use it just as much as me.

CATH: Yes.

PHIL: You *used* to use it just as much as me.

CATH: However…

PHIL: When it had two wheels.

CATH: Let's not talk about the wheels.

PHIL: No.

CATH: So.

PHIL: So. *(Pause.)* In fact we both know perfectly well what this is all about.

CATH: Do we?

PHIL: It happens every time I go in there.

CATH: Oh, you mean your little hidey-hole?

PHIL: I mean my workspace.

CATH: I mean your workspace.

PHIL: But I thought we'd *agreed*.

CATH: Yes! Fine! Get right back in there and pull the curtain again!

PHIL: What we agreed, if you remember…

CATH: I think it's completely mad!

PHIL: Yes, but what we agreed…

CATH: But if you can't stand the sight of me then why don't you just move in there for good and never come out?

PHIL: What we agreed…

CATH: You and Eric's chair together.

PHIL: What we agreed…

CATH: I should have thought it was a little bit *inauthentic*…

PHIL: Never mind inauthentic.

CATH: How about the *natural order?*

PHIL: What?

CATH: The natural order of the universe.

PHIL: I don't know what you're talking about.

CATH: No.

PHIL: What we agreed… *(Pause.)*

CATH: Go on, then!

PHIL: Is that we both needed a little personal space. *(Pause.)* Yes?

CATH: Personal space?

PHIL: Oh, come on.

CATH: Personal space…

PHIL: No need to say it like that. They're both perfectly common words. "Personal"—yes? "Space"—right?

CATH: Fine. Very… authentic.

PHIL: I don't know what you're complaining about.

CATH: I'm not complaining.

PHIL: You've got *your* space.

CATH: *My* space?

PHIL: The bathroom!

CATH: The bathroom? *You* use the bathroom!

PHIL: Yes, and *you* can use *my* space!

CATH: Sit behind that curtain? I don't want to sit behind that curtain! I think sitting behind that curtain is about as sane as putting a paper bag over your head and thinking no one can see you! *(Pause.)*

PHIL: Anyway, the relevant fact is that we agreed. Yes?

CATH: Personal space.

PHIL: Just as we also agreed about the bicycle.

CATH: We didn't agree about the bicycle.

PHIL: We agreed that it couldn't stay out on the pavement, because if it did then the other wheel would go as well. Yes?

CATH: I agreed that it couldn't stay on the *pavement*…

PHIL: You agreed that it couldn't stay on the *pavement*. Yes. You also agreed…

CATH: I didn't agree to keep it in here!

PHIL: You also agreed that it couldn't go in the hall downstairs, or else Pat would fall over it and break her leg, and then she wouldn't be able to come up here and drop in on us at all hours of the day and night, which would be a tragic loss to both of us.

CATH: I didn't agree to keep it in here, though!

PHIL: But there isn't anywhere else!

CATH: So?

PHIL: So, logically…

CATH: I thought we agreed you weren't going to say *logically?*

PHIL: Logically…

CATH: Let's forget the bicycle.

PHIL: Logically we must have agreed it was coming in here.

CATH: Yes, yes, yes. Fine. Wonderful. Just so long as it's not in *my* bit.

PHIL: All right. Just so long as you agree that we did agree…

CATH: Yes. I've said. Yes. So you go back in there, I'll go back in there… *(She goes to the bathroom. He has not moved.)* Now what?

PHIL: *Your* bit? What do you mean, *your* bit?

CATH: Round my side of the bed.

PHIL: Oh, that's *your* bit, is it?

CATH: *Now* what's going on?

PHIL: I didn't know you had a special bit of the room.

CATH: It's not special. It's simply my side of the bed. What's wrong with that?

PHIL: When was that decided?

CATH: It wasn't decided. It's always been my side of the bed.

PHIL: Always been your side of the bed?

CATH: I thought so.

PHIL: I didn't know that.

CATH: What do you mean, you didn't know that?

PHIL: I mean I didn't know that.

CATH: Personal space.

PHIL: Not in *here!*

CATH: Why not?

PHIL: This is common space! That's the point! Personal space—personal space—common space!

CATH: You've got your bit.

PHIL: No, I haven't.

CATH: Yes, you have.

PHIL: Where?

CATH: Round your side of the bed.

PHIL: This? I don't think of this as my bit.

CATH: Yes, you do.

PHIL: I *do* think of this as my bit?

CATH: Of course you do.

PHIL: How do you know what I think?

CATH: Because if you find anything of mine there you shout What's this thing doing round my side of the bed? *(Pause.)*

PHIL: So where does your bit stop?

CATH: Here.

PHIL: Here. There's a line, is there?

CATH: We don't need a line. We both know.

PHIL: Oh, we both know, do we?

CATH: Of course we know.

PHIL: You mean *you* know?

CATH: I mean we both know.

PHIL: You keep telling me what I know!

CATH: Because you don't seem to know.

PHIL: I don't know what I know?

CATH: Look, I've got things to do.

PHIL: Let me just get this straight. All this is yours? Yes? Over this piece of floor here you have absolute sovereignty. And the boundary of your territory is an imaginary line extending from the foot of the bed. While all *this,* up to an imaginary line from the foot of the bed on this side, is mine, to have and hold at my own good pleasure, to lease out, sell, burn, put to pasture or develop as building plots, at my own absolute discretion.

CATH: Phil, why are you behaving like this?

PHIL: I'm not behaving like anything. I'm trying, in an absolutely un-contentious way, to codify what seems to have become accepted practice, so that we both know where we stand. Now, these two areas apart, is all the rest of the room subject to mutual agreement or not?

CATH: As far as *I* know.

PHIL: As far as *you* know. Good.

CATH: Well, *isn't* it?

PHIL: As far as *I* know, yes. Though whether I *know* how far I know...

CATH: Let's just say yes. Yes, it is.

PHIL: Yes. All right. Yes?

CATH: Yes. *(Pause.)* Just so long as no more things suddenly vanish into things.

PHIL: Cath, for the last time! *(He snatches up the toy dog.)* It wasn't *me* who put this thing in the thing!

CATH: I know. It was *us*. It's not *you* waving it around. Not *my* face we're waving it in. *Our* face.

PHIL: You *don't* want to talk sensibly—we *won't* talk. *(He throws the dog down, returns to the alcove, and draws the curtain. Pause.)*

CATH: Oh. All right. Fine by me. I'll talk to myself. *(She sits down.)* Right. Who am I? *(Pause.)* Anyone else playing? Yes? No...? Never mind. So—who am I? Male? Yes. Real? Yes. Human? Half. *(Pause.)* Someone we both know? Yes. Pat? No—male—I *said*. Someone nice? No. Someone with a foul temper? Yes... How many's that?

PHIL: *(Off.)* Seven.

CATH: Seven, right... Am I... someone who's always trying to talk to people when they're in the bathroom? Yes. Am I... someone who screams at people if they leave the bathroom door half-open, then screams at them if they don't? Yes. *(Pause.)* Someone who always waits for someone else to make up quarrels? Yes. Anyone want to make a guess...? *(Pause.)*

PHIL: *(Off.)* Adolf Hitler.

CATH: Right. *(She gets up and opens the curtain.)* Come on, love... *(He closes the curtain.)* Oh, stay in there, then! Stay in there for good! Don't come out at all!

THE HOUSE ON
LAKE DESOLATION

Brian Christopher Williams

1 Man, 1 Woman
   Iggy (17) a disillusioned young man on the verge of self-destruction, and Janna (30) a black police officer trying to save his life.

Scene: A movie billboard in Los Angeles

Iggy, a hate-filled white supremacist, has traveled all the way to LA in hopes of being on hand for a race war. When he realizes that LA is just another big city in which he is the bottom of the heap, he tries to kill himself by climbing up a billboard with a gun. Here, Janna does her best to talk Iggy down.

                    O   O   O

(Lights rise to reveal Iggy, bleary-eyed and exhausted, seated shirtless on the ledge of a movie billboard in Los Angeles. There is a swastika still dripping with blood, etched into the flesh over his heart. He spins the chamber of the pistol and holds it to his head. He pulls the trigger. That chamber is blank. The billboard extends off into the SR wings, from which Janna, a thirty-year-old black police officer, now carefully shuffles toward Iggy. He looks up at her. She stops.)

JANNA: Hi.

IGGY: Hi.

JANNA: How ya doin'?

IGGY: Oh I'm fine. *(He spins the chamber and points it to his head.)*

JANNA: Don't. *(He turns to her.)*

IGGY: Why?

JANNA: I'm up for review next week and if I lose you it's not gonna look good for me. *(Iggy manages a little smile and puts the gun down in his lap.)* I don't have a gun. I'm just here to talk. I'm gonna sit down now, okay?

IGGY: Help yourself. *(He points the gun at the ledge, indicating a seat.)*

JANNA: Don't point that at me.

IGGY: I'm not going to shoot you.

JANNA: They don't know that.

IGGY: Who?

JANNA: Those guys down there with their guns trained on you.

IGGY: What kind of sense does that make? I've got a gun pointed at my head and they're down there to do what? Finish me off if I should happen to miss?

JANNA: No one wants to see you do that.

IGGY: Of course they do. They'd be praying for it if I was cruising up the thruway in a white Ford Bronco.

JANNA: I'm Janna. What's your name?

IGGY: Benito.

JANNA: What do your friends call you?

IGGY: Il Duce.

JANNA: What are you doin' up here, Benito?

IGGY: The air was just a little too thick down on Sunset Boulevard. I thought I'd come up for a little breeze. *(Pointing.)* That's where John Belushi bought the farm, isn't it?

JANNA: You know, I'm a little scared of heights. What do you say we climb down—

IGGY: Who are you kidding? I get down to the street, you'll slap on some cuffs and truck me off to prison.

JANNA: You been to prison, Benito?

IGGY: Some of my closest allies are in prison. *(He raises the gun to his head.)*

JANNA: How long you been here from New York? *(He lowers the gun, genuinely surprised.)*

IGGY: How'd you know I'm from New York?

JANNA: White Ford Bronco on the thruway. We call them freeways here.

IGGY: Impressive.

JANNA: How'd you get here?

IGGY: You'd be surprised how cooperative strangers can be when they know you're carrying a loaded weapon.

JANNA: Why'd you come to LA?

IGGY: You know, television can be very misleading.

JANNA: You wanted to be on television?

IGGY: The 11:00 news. I came for the race wars. I was promised race wars.

JANNA: Ah. Does it bother you that I'm black?

IGGY: Not anymore.

JANNA: Oh no?

IGGY: I'm an equal-opportunity hater now. Jews, blacks, Mexicans, even whites. I hate everyone.

JANNA: I was admiring the artwork there on your chest.

IGGY: You like that?

JANNA: Impressive.

IGGY: You know, Charlie Manson has one right here on his fore-head.

JANNA: But yours is on your chest.

IGGY: Over my soul. See Charlie, he had it all wrong. That's why he ended up in prison. He was screwed up in the head, that's why he put the spider on his mind instead of his heart. He hated and it was all in his head.

JANNA: But not you?

IGGY: No.

JANNA: You hate with your soul?

IGGY: No. I hate my soul.

JANNA: You know, Benito, I would really hate for something to happen to you.

IGGY: I know. You've got a review coming up.

JANNA: I was kidding about that. I like you. I want to help you.

IGGY: Do you believe in reincarnation?

JANNA: I don't know.

IGGY: I met this girl on the street this week. Her head was shaved and she wore loose clothes and sandals. She took me to this lit-tle house where about a dozen of 'em lived, boys and girls just like her. And they let me take a shower and they fed me. And when I was done eating, this girl kneeled down on the floor next to where I was sitting and she stared into my eyes. And she told me that we had known each other in a past life, that we'd been drawn together again in this lifetime in order to work out some sort of mess that we didn't get right in the last go round. *(He turns to face Janna, who is listening to him intently.)* So I shot her. *(Beat. He starts laughing.)* Lighten up. I'm just kidding.

JANNA: So you've got to work it out, Benito. That's what that girl was telling you. You've got to stick around and make it work this time around.

IGGY: So I started thinking. Wouldn't it be nice to start from scratch? Wouldn't it be great to just chuck this whole mess and start from the very beginning, diapers and all that crap? Maybe I'd get born into a big family with lots of brothers and sisters. And a mom that cooked pot roast on Sundays and lived to be 100. And a dad who played football with us kids, both the boys and girls. Maybe next time I could be one of the Kennedys.

JANNA: Maybe next time you'll be born Jewish. Or black. Or Mexican. I don't know about all that reincarnation stuff, Benito. All I know is today. Every single day you've got the opportunity to make your life whatever you want it to be.

IGGY: There comes a point where you can't go back.

JANNA: I'm not talking going back. I'm talking future. Look at what you did. You didn't like your life in New York, so you picked up and came all the way to Los Angeles. You don't like it here, you can go somewhere else, anywhere else, Hawaii, Europe. Hell, you can go to the moon if you want to. You can do anything you want to do. You've got your whole life in front of you. This life. Here. Now. Don't throw that away.

IGGY: I don't like this life here, now. I haven't liked it for a very long time.

JANNA: Then change it. But don't go this way. Suicide's the coward's way out. *(Iggy thinks about this for a moment. He starts laughing.)* What's funny?

IGGY: I am a coward. *(He laughs.)* This gun doesn't have any bullets. *(He laughs loudly.)*

JANNA: Really? *(Iggy nods. He spins the chamber and fires at his head. Empty chamber. He spins again and fires at his head. Empty chamber.)* Come on, Benito. Let's climb down.

IGGY: I don't want to go to prison.

JANNA: That's not gonna happen.

IGGY: I don't want to go to prison.

JANNA: You won't. We'll climb down. We'll have a doctor look at that wound.

IGGY: My soul.

JANNA: Yes. We'll get you fixed up. We'll take care of you. I promise. *(Iggy nods slowly. Janna rises to her feet.)* C'mon. Let's go. *(Iggy nods. He rises to his feet. He is transfixed on the crowd beneath him.)*

IGGY: There are a lot of people down there.

JANNA: They're all concerned about you.

IGGY: They have guns.

JANNA: They won't hurt you. I promise. *(Iggy turns to face her. She is smiling at him. Slowly he raises his gun and points it at her. Realizing what is about to happen, she shouts to the crowd beneath them.)* Don't shoot. *(Blackout. From the darkness, there is a round of gunfire.)*

HUNTERS OF THE SOUL

Marion Isaac McClinton

1 Man, 1 Woman
Sylvester (20s) a young black man, and Hazel (40s) his mother.

Scene: Here and Now

Hazel is a woman struggling to cope with her dysfunctional family and the harsh inner-city world in which they live. Following the death of her ex-husband—a man she could never stop loving—Hazel finds herself sinking into a pit of grief and despair. Here, she describes her state to Sylvester, her streetwise son.

○   ○   ○

SYLVESTER: Mother?

HAZEL: Yes.

SYLVESTER: You want me to wipe off your face?

HAZEL: Don't bother.

SYLVESTER: Ya know… hindsight's a bitch and it never changes anything.

HAZEL: I don't know. I don't know anything like that at all. I used to know things. The things that I'd remember. Not like I wanted them to be but how I remembered them. How they were. Actually. You know I'm sure there was a time back when I was living in the world when I knew the right answers. Not only that but probably knew what the right questions were too. Knew both before anybody ever thought them. Don't have any now. Questions, answers, nothing.

SYLVESTER: You know how much you gonna miss me when I'm gone? Who else gonna listen to you talking and care what you say? Crazy or not sounding, and treat it like it just come from John the Baptist. Who? You know how much you gonna miss me when I'm gone?

HAZEL: Yes, I do. Do you? *(Pause.)*

SYLVESTER: Guess I never thought about you... you know... before...

HAZEL: The funny thing is that I've been thinking about a lot of things that stretch back to before I can remember. I have an idea about it now. It was something that always lived someplace else. Never came knocking at my door before. Ain't that the way? Get a reservation on the boat and the river dries up. My memory just woke up one morning and died. Didn't understand it at first. Just was shocked something like that could happen.

SYLVESTER: Mother?

HAZEL: Was so tough. Coming back. Death all around, just lurking. Waiting to bring back everything that scared me to the marrow of my bones. Froze my soul. Didn't bother to send me back to myself. Just sent back bits and pieces. Didn't remember about nothing from anything before. Had forgotten how to. Just saw from before I could remember. Don't believe I recognized a single thing through.

SYLVESTER: Would you like something to eat?

HAZEL: Is it time already?

SYLVESTER: Been time already. You want me to cook you something or to send out?

HAZEL: I might want to see somebody. Who I don't know.

SYLVESTER: I can take you out. I don't mind.

HAZEL: Didn't we just eat?

SYLVESTER: When? Now?

HAZEL: Just now. Right this instant.

SYLVESTER: You okay?

HAZEL: I don't think so. I could have sworn...

SYLVESTER: You ain't ate since we buried Dad.

HAZEL: And when...

SYLVESTER: A couple of days ago.

HAZEL: Exactly. Be exact.

SYLVESTER: Three days ago. It was exactly three days ago.

HAZEL: Thank you. That explains it.

SYLVESTER: What?

HAZEL: Everything. *(Pause.)*

SYLVESTER: I really think you should try to eat something, Mother.

HAZEL: I just ate.

SYLVESTER: Whatever.

HAZEL: What a marvelous thought.

SYLVESTER: What, Mother?

HAZEL: Whatever. There are still things possible with that word. The territory is still wide open.

SYLVESTER: I think I'll turn on the TV.

HAZEL: I'm not sure but I think it was a while ago. Back when I had the shining. Did you know I used to have the shining?

SYLVESTER: I think you should eat something before you walk into a McDonald's and blow everybody in there away from hunger. I know that.

HAZEL: I can remember back to when I could heal people by just laying my hands on them. I had medicine in my soul. I could make blind men see by rubbing their tears in my eyes. I could suck the cancer out of somebody's chest by laying my head on their heart. I had the shining so strong my name had to be Luster.

SYLVESTER: Luster was Dad's last name, Mother. You weren't born to it. You married it.

HAZEL: It was my destiny to have that name. I had more Luster in me than all the gold in Fort Knox. Ain't nobody had the shining more than me. Now nothing shines. Everything just dull. Not even enough light for the darkness to want to come. My memory just gone into a hole and it won't come out.

SYLVESTER: You just tired and ain't slept.

HAZEL: I'm in a hole, Sylvester. A hole of grief. I ain't sure I'm getting out of it either.

SYLVESTER: There ain't no holes around here, pal.

HAZEL: There are a whole lotta of them around here. Some on the outside and some are on the inside. You drowning in one right now.

SYLVESTER: Me? I'm fine. I'm just trying to live in the world.

HAZEL: How do you know that?

SYLVESTER: Mother… I am sorry you are so torn up by this. I don't
get it, but I can see it and I feel for you. But I ain't hurt that bad
by it all. I ain't walking around like I got hit in the head by a
Coke bottle. Let's not make him out to be more than he was.
He wasn't that much.

HAZEL: How can you say that?

SYLVESTER: He was a bum, Momma, Dad was a bum. I'm a thief, he
was a bum. Momma face it, ain't nobody turned out that well.
Even your respectable kids ain't nothing but boot lickers.

HAZEL: I AM NOT YOUR MOMMA! I AM YOUR MOTHER! I AIN'T
NOBODY'S DAMN MOMMA!

SYLVESTER: I ain't meant nothing by nothing, Mother, I just said…

HAZEL: These kids running around the streets calling their mothers
momma this and mammy that! Bunch of conkhead thieving
punks is what they are! The whole lot of them.

SYLVESTER: Nobody wears conks, mother. You getting it confused
with jherri curls.

HAZEL: I DON'T CARE WHAT THEY CALL WHAT'S ON THEIR HEAD,
I WON'T HAVE YOU CALLING ME ANYTHING THAT COMES
INTO YOUR HEAD! WHATEVER PLEASES YOU! I WILL NOT
HAVE IT! NOT IN THIS HOUSE! NOT IN MY HOME! YOU MIGHT
NOT RESPECT MUCH BUT YOU WILL RESPECT THAT! I WILL DIE
THE DEATH OF THREE DOGS IN THE STREET BEFORE I LET YOU
DISRESPECT ME TOTALLY WHERE I LIVE! I BROUGHT YOUR
BLACK ASS INTO THIS WORLD, I CAN TAKE YOUR BLACK BE-
HIND OUT OF IT TOO! AND ME AND YOUR DADDY CAN MAKE
ANOTHER ONE JUST LIKE YOU! *(Pause.)* Can't you feel nothing?

SYLVESTER: I'm sorry.

HAZEL: Don't you respect anything?

SYLVESTER: I respect you.

HAZEL: You respect me sometimes. Your daddy had respect for me.

SYLVESTER: Man, love sure is blind. He had a funny way of showing
it.

HAZEL: He knew I was the mother of his children, not somebody's
damn momma. He respected that more than you do.

SYLVESTER: He didn't respect the bed of his wife, did he? He didn't respect that for a damn second. And it didn't exactly matter with who he was disrespecting you, did it?

HAZEL: The man loved me. He was just sick.

SYLVESTER: Yeah, he was a real romantic kind of fellow, wasn't he?

HAZEL: I got to know him real good over his lifetime. Got to see the whipmarks all over his soul. Welts hardened in there and wouldn't be bled. He got all swallowed up by it.

SYLVESTER: By what?

HAZEL: Life with a capital "F."

SYLVESTER: I don't think I'm going for that.

HAZEL: Why should you? Why should you care?

SYLVESTER: I wouldn't be here if I didn't. What else is the attraction to this joint? Great childhood memories? Bullshit! Wasn't nothing great to remember about nothing. I wish I could go back to before I could remember. I wish I could just go back there and not have to care about anyone. *(Pause.)*

HAZEL: You hate everything so much? Yourself? Me? You hate that much? How can you stand it. I'm holding on to what little I got left to hold on to, but I won't hold on to that. Deliberate hate, deliberate cruelty, I won't never stoop that low that I gotta grab hold of things like that. I'll sink before I'll stand on a foundation of hate and cruelty.

SYLVESTER: I'm not cruel.

HAZEL: You ain't the opposite of it.

SYLVESTER: What do you want from me? I'm here! I stay in this house with you! I am concerned about what happens to you in this house.

HAZEL: You might stay in this house with me, you might even be concerned, but you ain't living with me in our home. Your concern don't translate to care, or love. It's duty and you know it.

SYLVESTER: All right, fuck it! Do what the fuck you want to do! Why don't you just keep filling up that glass and let the whiskey take care of everything. Drink yourself to death. A slow black dying death. Get struck by a bolt of lightning, let a brick safe drop on your head, I don't care! Why should I? It ain't never gonna be enough. Who I am, not who you want me to be, is never gonna be enough. Just fuck it! I'm out of here. I should have been gone.

HAZEL: Come here.

SYLVESTER: I'm sick of this, Mother.

HAZEL: Please. *(Sylvester goes over to Hazel. She slaps the ever-loving shit out of him.)* I told you about all that cussing in my face.

SYLVESTER: (Okay.)

HAZEL: You will respect me. No matter how much of a shell I am of what I used to be. You will respect me and my house. You want to be a man of respect? A bad man that has a town in fear of his name? Then why don't you change your diapers, stop acting like a little colored boy and find out what it is to be a man. Instead of somebody who gets slapped around in his own neighborhood. On the street he grew up on. *(Pause.)* You on the down escalator to nowhere fast, boy.

SYLVESTER: All right. Correct. I can't argue with you.

HAZEL: I'm sorry, but that's the way it is.

THE KENTUCKY CYCLE

Robert Schenkkan

1 Man, 1 Woman
Star (30s) a Cherokee woman kidnapped by Michael Rowen with the express purpose of providing him with an heir, and Patrick (16) their son.

Scene: The Rowen homestead in Eastern Kentucky, 1792

Sixteen years before, Star was taken captive from her tribe by the brutal Michael Rowen, who severed the tendon in her heel so she couldn't run away. She has since resigned herself to life with the arrogant man. Their son, Patrick, has fallen in love with a girl on a neighboring farm, and here asks his mother for help in courting her.

O   O   O

(Dusk. The front yard of the Rowen house. The original single room has been expanded. Among other additions is a simple front porch and steps. The house and yard are bare and unadorned, strictly functional. There is a pile of logs on the porch and an old axe. In the yard is a tin tub, partially filled with water. Patrick enters, cradling his rifle and a leather bag containing a pair of dead rabbits. Star limps in, carrying two wooden buckets full of water. She stops and looks at Patrick.)

STAR: *Ostas hindhalid?* [Good hunting?]

PATRICK: Couple of rabbits. Here, gimme those, Ma. *(He throws his bag on the porch, lays his rifle down and takes the buckets from her. He pours them into the tub.)*

STAR: *To hi ju?* [How are you?]

PATRICK: I'm fine.

STAR: It embarrasses you now to speak the language of your grandfathers?

PATRICK: No. It don't embarrass me. I just don't see the point.

STAR: Not to forget who you are, that is the point.

PATRICK: Not much danger of that around here, is there? *(Beat.)*

STAR: I'll bring your supper out. Cooler on the porch. *(He sits. She goes in, returns with a bowl of food. She picks up the rabbits while he eats.)*

PATRICK: Good.

STAR: Took you all day to get these? Losin' your touch.

PATRICK: Didn't take me all… *(Before he can finish protesting, Star goes inside with the rabbits. She returns.)* Most of the mornin' I sat up on the ridge.

STAR: Oh. Corn gonna plant itself this year?

PATRICK: I finished that piece on the Shilling.

STAR: Uh-huh. What's on the ridge worth a visit?

PATRICK: Nothin'. Just did me some thinkin'.

STAR: Alone? *(Beat.)*

PATRICK: Mostly.

STAR: I knew when that Talbert girl come sniffin' round here this mornin' you wasn't gonna get a lick of work done.

PATRICK: I planted the damn field!

STAR: Don't curse in front of your ma.

PATRICK: Don't see what you got against the Talberts. From what I hear you're a regular visitor over there. *(Beat.)*

STAR: What is it you hear?

PATRICK: You doctored her Pa.

STAR: His name is Joseph.

PATRICK: Joseph? Michael know about it?

STAR: What do you think?

PATRICK: I think he hears about it, he'll skin you alive.

STAR: Are you gonna tell him? *(Beat.)* Folks think I have the Gift for healin' and readin' dreams. Because I'm different. Because I'm Cherokee. Michael laughs, but as long as they pay, he laughs to himself. I think, why should he have all this money? Why not my son? And so, when I can, I see people secretly. Like Joseph.

PATRICK: For me?

STAR: Someday you'll want land of your own. A woman of your own.

PATRICK: Why hide it from me?

STAR: So if Michael finds out, he'll be angry only with me. *(Beat. He crosses over and hugs her knees, puts his head in her lap.)*

PATRICK: *Do yu jiskanoqi. Skidoliga?* [I am sorry. Forgive me?] *(She kisses him on the top of his head, strokes his hair roughly.)*

STAR: *I gvkewidina.* [It is forgotten.] You want this Ruth Talbert?

PATRICK: Rebecca.

STAR: Whatever. What she wants, you can give her easy enough. You don't have to marry her for that.

PATRICK: She ain't like that.

STAR: I see. Maybe she's smarter than I thought.

PATRICK: I love her.

STAR: You love her. Now. Today, you love her. But tomorrow? Next year? Chuji. Why so much hurry? Why marry her? *(Beat.)*

PATRICK: If I marry her, maybe her pa'd gimme that piece of bottom land next to ours. *(She cuffs him.)*

STAR: You are your father's son. Truly.

PATRICK: Not so's he'd notice.

STAR: I never understand this. What you two have is never enough. You work from sunrise to sunset and you can't plow all what you have now, but you want *more.* More *land!* Why?

PATRICK: It's the only thing that lasts. *(Beat.)*

STAR: You live like that, Chuji, you live a lonely life.

PATRICK: Somethin' different.

STAR: Everybody gotta right to some happiness, *osta* Chuji. You gotta right.

PATRICK: She makes me happy. Rebecca. *(Beat.)* You help me?

STAR: How?

PATRICK: Talk to him for me. 'Bout us. *(She walks to the tub, runs her hand through the water.)*

STAR: Michael don't listen to me.

PATRICK: He's comin' back. *(She hesitates.)*

STAR: You seen him?

PATRICK: This mornin'.

STAR: You sure?

PATRICK: Somebody was movin' thru the gap in a hurry.

STAR: Coulda been anybody.

PATRICK: Who?

STAR: When'll he get here?

PATRICK: Tonight mebbe. Tomorrow for sure. But tonight I think. *(Beat.)* You could tell him… tell him that Talbert bottom land'd give us a third agin as much.

STAR: It'd give your *pa* a third agin as much. *(She takes his bowl and starts into the house.)*

PATRICK: Same thing. It's all gonna come down to me, innit?

STAR: Is it? *(She sits on the porch. Patrick stares at her in confusion.)*

PATRICK: What're you talkin' 'bout?

STAR: I'm not sayin' nothin'. Said too much already. *(Preoccupied, she absentmindedly strokes her injured leg.)*

PATRICK: Your leg botherin' you a lot? *(She shrugs. Looks off into the woods where Michael is.)* Here. Lemme rub it for you. *(He sits next to her. She hikes up her skirt and swings her leg into his lap. He begins to knead her scarred calf. She leans back against a post, her eyes closed.)* What'd you mean about… about the land not comin' to me. I'm his only son.

STAR: Are you?

PATRICK: What d'you mean, "Are you?"—"Is it?" You know somethin' why don't you just say it, 'stead of dancin' around!

STAR: Lower.

PATRICK: What?

STAR: Rub lower. *(He does so.)* What does Michael do in Louisville?

PATRICK: I don't know.

STAR: Home come?

PATRICK: 'Cause I ain't never been.

STAR: How come?

PATRICK: 'Cause I gotta stay here and take care of things! *(Beat.)*

STAR: He got a woman down there.

PATRICK: How do you know?

STAR: I seen her in a dream.

PATRICK: You seen her?

STAR: Blue eyes, corn-silk hair. She always be crossin' a muddy river in my dreams.

PATRICK: Muddy water? That's death. *(She nods.)* Mebbe she's dead already.

STAR: Mebbe.

PATRICK: What I care if he got some woman down there? Specially if she's dead now.

STAR: Mebbe she had him a baby.

PATRICK: He… got him another family down there?

STAR: Why else he always got to go alone? You a growned man, Chuji. With your help, he could pack in twice as much on these trips. You ever knowed Michael to turn his back on a dollar? How come he don't take you?

PATRICK: You seen the baby in your dream?

STAR: Clear as the bottom of the Shillin'.

PATRICK: Boy or girl?

STAR: She give him a *son.*

PATRICK: A son!

STAR: Where does that leave you?

PATRICK: I'd still be the oldest! It'd all still come to me! That's the law!

STAR: Law? *(She laughs.)* Michael ever pay a whole lotta mind to the *law?*

PATRICK: Why wouldn't he let me have my share?

STAR: You know why.

PATRICK: Why!

STAR: 'Cause he hates you.

PATRICK: That's a lie!

STAR: Look me in the face and tell me it is! *(He can't.)*

PATRICK: Why? Why's he hate me? Nothin' I ever do is right. Never has been. He looks at me like I was some kinda mad dog, gonna tear somethin' precious away from him.

STAR: He's afraid of you.

PATRICK: Afraid?! Hell, Michael Rowen ain't afraid of nothin'!

STAR: Look at yourself, Chuji, *look!* See yourself as you really *are*— not like that hungry dog he turns you into, the one who whines and licks the hand that beats him. You are bigger than him now. And stronger. He sees you and he feels old. He feels tired. He sees *death* in you. That's how you scare him, Chuji, and that's why he hates you. Because there is no forgiving that. And that's why he will never give you your rightful share of this land. *Your* land. Not till you bury him innit! *(Beat.)* Ask him. You don't believe me? Ask him for your share and see what he says.

ONE MAN'S DANCE

Aaron Levy

1 Man, 1 Woman
Ira and Rebeka (both 18) childhood friends on the verge of something much bigger.

Scene: Here and Now

As they both prepare for their freshman year at college, these two old friends make an important discovery about their feelings for one another.

O   O   O

REBEKA: Whoa! Ira! Did you see that one?! I just saw one—hurry up, make a wish! Hurry!

IRA: Okay, I wish that no bats come and eat Rebeka Blau and me—

REBEKA: You can't say it out loud, stupid.

IRA: *(Whispers.)* I wish that no bats come and eat— *(Rebeka slaps him playfully in the stomach.)*

REBEKA: Shhh! I'm wishing.

IRA: Fine. Wish. But I don't see how a piece of light a million years away is gonna know what the hell you're thinkin'.

REBEKA: You ever done it outside?

IRA: What?

REBEKA: You heard me. Have you ever done it outside?

IRA: Yeah, well, that's personal. We agreed we wouldn't talk about that kind of stuff a long time ago.

REBEKA: Why, though? I mean, I've known you longer than anybody. And we're about to kind of part for awhile, "go find ourselves" or whatever. What's there to hide?

IRA: Nothing.

REBEKA: I'm more than willing to share my history with you.

IRA: I've heard enough about your sex life from other people, and I can't say that I get off on that type of thing.

REBEKA: Hey, I don't sleep around, Ira! You know that!

IRA: Yeah, I know that…

REBEKA: Well, 'cause I don't… sometimes I wish I did, or could, but when it comes right down to it, I don't.

IRA: What about Joey Harris?

REBEKA: *(Pause, looks at him.)* That's not to say I'm a virgin, 'cause, 'cause I'm not. Although sometimes, I consider that I may be, you know, unofficially…

IRA: Uh-huh.

REBEKA: Yeah, I slept with him! Okay, yeah, more than once too…

IRA: Rebeka, please! I'm not having fun anymore!

REBEKA: Well, what was I supposed to do? Huh? Wait? *(Beat. Looks up.)* I never did it with him outside, though. What about you? Margie Krisminski?

IRA: Hey I don't kiss and tell, Rebeka, it's just not my style.

REBEKA: Ah, I guess it's Margie's style then. How was she, Ira? Were you attracted to her breasts or her personality?

IRA: No.

REBEKA: Well, what? I know you had sex with her!

IRA: Once. Only once. Okay? And I didn't even like it. I mean I liked it, but I didn't like her.

REBEKA: You didn't like her?

IRA: One time, and I didn't even like her.

REBEKA: If you didn't like her, why did you have sex with her?

IRA: 'Cause. 'Cause she'd been after me for awhile. I mean she was all over me at Chelsie Brown's Halloween party last year.

REBEKA: Oh. So, she'd been after you for a while? A-huh. It's starting to make sense now. Yup, it all makes perfect fucking sense now.

IRA: Stop sayin' fuck, Rebeka.

REBEKA: Why?! Why do you always tell me to stop cussin'?! Huh?!

IRA: 'Cause you're a pretty girl, when you start cussin' you don't look pretty anymore… at least to me you don't.

REBEKA: Well, it's not like I have to worry about being attractive to you anyway.

IRA: What's that supposed to mean?

REBEKA: Means what it means. Oh, don't look at me like I hurt every one of your little feelings. Look, ever since we went through puberty, and before that even, I've always flirted with you—trying to create a comfortable environment for you to, you know, express your masculinity...

IRA: Express my masculinity?

REBEKA: Put a move on me, Ira?

IRA: Oh... I didn't know that's what you were doing—

REBEKA: Oh, c'mon! A girl asks you to the prom like every year, you could take a hint.

IRA: I just don't dance, Rebeka, like I told you—

REBEKA: It's okay, Ira! I know. And it's okay.

IRA: You know?

REBEKA: Yes, and I want you to know I still accept you.

IRA: *(Confused.)* Thanks—

REBEKA: I kind of think it's neat. And you should know and realize that you're not alone. In fact most really good artistic-type people are gay too—

IRA: What?!

REBEKA: Don't get me wrong, for awhile I used to think it was just me—

IRA: Hold it, let's backtrack a sec—

REBEKA: But then when you started acting distant, like when I started dating Joey real serious *(Laughs.)* and I actually thought maybe you were jealous of Joey 'cause you liked me—

IRA: That's not it—

REBEKA: But then I realized you were actually attracted to Joey, and who wouldn't be, male or female, but—

IRA: Rebeka!

REBEKA: Anyway, I just want you to know that I still accept you. I mean, I'm not homophobic or nothin'— *(Ira fully embraces her with a kiss. Then he gently pushes her away as they disembrace.)*

IRA: There! There, okay?! Okay?! I'm not gay! *(Pause, softer.)* I'm really not.

REBEKA: *(Dreamy, almost whoosy.)* Whoa...

IRA: What? What's wrong, Rebeka?

REBEKA: Wow.

IRA: Sorry.

REBEKA: You've got some amazing lips.

IRA: *(Embarrassed and shocked, rambling.)* Well, you remember I used to play the trumpet in Junior High, kinda works the lip muscles... *(Rebeka kisses him now, even longer and more passionate. Ira is stunned afterwards.)* Happy Birthday, Rebeka...

REBEKA: *(Laughs.)* Ira, it's not my birthday, it's yours... are you all right?

IRA: *(Pause.)* I, I've never kissed a girl like that before. *(Beat.)* I've never kissed a boy like that before either. *(Beat.)* Well, I've never wanted to... but I have always, always, as long as I can remember, wanted to kiss you.

REBEKA: Well, it's about fucking time.

IRA: Now what? I mean, in a month—

REBEKA: I guess we'll see then won't we?

PADDYWACK

Daniel Magee

1 Man, 1 Woman

Damien (20–30) a young Irishman who may or may not be an IRA terrorist, and Annette (20–30) an Englishwoman who is attracted to him.

Scene: London

Damien has arrived in England allegedly to find better work than he can at home in Belfast. He is befriended by Colin, an upper-class Englishman who is temporarily living in the same flophouse as part of a sociological study. The two meet Colin's girlfriend, Annette, at a local pub and proceed to close it down. Here, they have returned to Annette's flat where Colin has passed out. Damien and Annette suddenly find themselves irresistibly drawn to one another.

O   O   O

(Cross fade lighting to Annette's flat. About an hour later. Colin has keeled over on the sofa and is sleeping. Annette is sitting at the other end of the same sofa. Damien is sitting at the table.)

DAMIEN: He wasn't kidding when he said he was knackered, was he? *(Nods towards Colin.)*

ANNETTE: *(Lifting her glass.)* Not to mention this stuff… He doesn't drink much.

DAMIEN: It was my fault really… I was a bit pushy about the carry-out.

ANNETTE: He could have said no…

DAMIEN: You reckon…?

ANNETTE: *(A bit bemused.)* What do you mean?

DAMIEN: Ah, nothing… *(Rises with the bottle and approaches her.)* Here, have a top up.

ANNETTE: No, I'm curious… What did you mean?

DAMIEN: Well, it's his nature, isn't it? … he's too kind… too good mannered.

ANNETTE: *(Fishing.)* You think so?

DAMIEN: Yeah, for his own good... He didn't want to let anybody down... Spoil the fun.

ANNETTE: Do you like him?

DAMIEN: Yeah, ...He's a nice bloke.

ANNETTE: Yes, but what do you *think* of him?

DAMIEN: *(Becomes wary.)* I thought I just answered that. *(Returns to sit.)*

ANNETTE: You did and you didn't... I like carrots but if you asked me what I thought about them, I'd say "bugger all."

DAMIEN: *(A little exasperated.)* Annette, I have the feeling that I'm being cross-questioned in pursuit of some end I'm not aware of...

ANNETTE: That's called paranoia, Damien.

DAMIEN: I know what it's called, Annette. Fear of heights is called vertigo but you don't get it until you're on the edge of a cliff...

ANNETTE: You feel you're on the edge of a cliff?

DAMIEN: I feel I'm on the edge of something... What's all this about Colin? ... one minute you're taking the piss out of him and the next... well with me anyway... you seem to be sort of protecting him... From what... *me?*

ANNETTE: *(She holds out her glass.)* Here... Refill, please.

DAMIEN: *(He does so.)* Yes?

ANNETTE: Since he's met you... *(Pause.)* he's changed... For the better in many ways. It's like he's on a sort of "high." He's more positive... enthusiastic... more full of life.

DAMIEN: *(Unsure how to react.)* Ummmm... That doesn't sound too bad.

ANNETTE: It isn't... in itself.

DAMIEN: So... What's the other side of the coin?

ANNETTE: *(Turns and looks at Colin.)* Look at him... that's Colin... a cuddly, good-hearted, loving... human being. *(She's struggling for expression and stops.)*

DAMIEN: *(Waits for a time. Almost whispers.)* Yes.

ANNETTE: *(More composed and without looking at Damien.)* That zoo you live in... If he strays too far into it... it'll devour him...

(Looks straight at Damien.)

DAMIEN: *(Quietly.)* Then, Annette… why don't you take him out of it?

ANNETTE: *(Surprised.)* Ha! …therein lies the rub… *(Pauses.)*

DAMIEN: *(Gently.)* I know.

ANNETTE: I expect *you* do.

DAMIEN: It's because of you he's there.

ANNETTE: *(Affectionately.)* Full marks, Mister clever cloggs.

DAMIEN: I knew it the minute I saw him… "There"… I says to me-self… "is a Dilemma Devil"

ANNETTE: A what?

DAMIEN: A "Dilemma Devil"? …Someone who seems to thrive on the horns of a dilemma, sort of hooked… there's another word for it.

ANNETTE: *(Wary.)* And what word would that be?

DAMIEN: The one that sticks in your throat.

ANNETTE: *(Tense.)* Say it.

DAMIEN: *(Looking steadily at Annette.)* A loser.

ANNETTE: That's a cruel thing to say.

DAMIEN: Is it? …Is it cruel to observe it, think it… or just to say it. Do you think that *I* am cruel?

ANNETTE: I don't know… I… expect you… could be…

DAMIEN: Do you want me to leave?

ANNETTE: *(Staring at him.)* No…

DAMIEN: You're very gracious… when we finish this bottle I'll hit the road.

ANNETTE: *(Still staring at him.)* He told me about you.

DAMIEN: He doesn't know anything about me to tell.

ANNETTE: Aren't you afraid that he knows… and that he told me?

DAMIEN: And what does he know?

ANNETTE: That you're politically involved.

DAMIEN: I can assure you, Annette, Colin hasn't seen me with so much as a leaflet.

ANNETTE: I'm sure of that.

DAMIEN: *(Small laugh.)* And what's that supposed to mean?

ANNETTE: I wouldn't think you'd be on the ballot box end of things.

DAMIEN: Oh, wouldn't you?

ANNETTE: No.

DAMIEN: So… what do *you* think I am?

ANNETTE: I don't know.

DAMIEN: Well everything's fine then, isn't it?

ANNETTE: Don't patronize me.

DAMIEN: And don't you be talking to me about things you know nothing about.

ANNETTE: I'm not Colin… He's a romantic… when he sees suffering… injustice… it hurts him and he feels he *has* to do something about it… The problem is he can't because he can't take the pain…

DAMIEN: What pain?

ANNETTE: The pain involved in really doing something about it. He thinks living in that horrible home is in some way a "statement" and, like you said, to "impress" me. The problem is, the more I tell him he should get out, the greater he thinks his "statement" …his pseudo-struggle… is. He…

DAMIEN: Annette… why are you telling me all this?

ANNETTE: Do you know, I'm not quite sure.

DAMIEN: Are you afraid I'll put you in the same boat as Colin?

ANNETTE: *(Flares.)* You arrogant bastard.

DAMIEN: Jesus, arrogant now… First it was cruel, now it's arrogant. I'm telling you, if they ever make a film about me they'll have to revive Hammer Studios and resuscitate Vincent Price to do the part.

ANNETTE: Ok I over-reacted… But you really *are* an arrogant bastard.

DAMIEN: I suppose I am a bit.

ANNETTE: *(Laughs.)* You are something else… tell me, what would this film be about?

DAMIEN: Well let me see… How about "The Life And Times Of The Man Who Threw Off The Yoke Of British Imperialism In Ireland By Going Over And Blowing The Living Bejasus Out Of England"… *(He looks at Annette who is taken aback and makes no response.)* You don't like the title… Too long?

ANNETTE: Isn't that a rather dangerous thing to say?

DAMIEN: *(Suddenly very serious.)* It depends upon who you say it to.

ANNETTE: So why did you say it to me?

DAMIEN: Because I knew you could take a joke.

ANNETTE: Some joke.

DAMIEN: Yeah, I know... It's had us in stitches in Ireland for over 300 years. *(He drains his glass and stands up.)* Well, that's the end of the whisky... I'll be hitting the road... Thanks for your hospitality. *(He stands over her and hands her is empty glass. She doesn't get up.)* Shall I be seeing you again?

ANNETTE: Yes.

PTERODACTYLS

Nicky Silver

1 Man, 2 Women
Todd (30s) HIV positive, Grace (50s) his mother, and Emma (20-30) his sister.

Scene: Here and Now

When Todd discovers that he has AIDS, he goes home to live with his family. Dysfunctionality reigns supreme when he makes his appearance.

O   O   O

TODD: Hello.

EMMA: (*Startled.*) What?!

TODD: I said hello.

EMMA: Where did you come from?

TODD: I walked from the train station.

EMMA: (*She is nervous and afraid of him.*) How did you get in here?

TODD: I just want to lie down.

EMMA: I asked you a question!

TODD: The door was open.

EMMA: That door is locked!

TODD: No, it's not.

EMMA: What do you want?

TODD: I need a place to live. I need a place to sleep. I've been traveling so long. I've been walking forever.

EMMA: Don't sit down!

TODD: Everything's different.

EMMA: What are you talking about?

TODD: The furniture's different.

EMMA: Different from what?

TODD: The sofa is new.

EMMA: Do you want money? Is that what you want?

TODD: I don't want any money.

EMMA: Why are you staring at me?

TODD: You look so different.

EMMA: Don't come at me—

TODD: You look beautiful.

EMMA: Get out of here!

TODD: Don't you recognize me?

EMMA: Just go please!

TODD: You don't remember me?

EMMA: We've never never met—

TODD: (*Approaching her.*) Of course we have.

EMMA: Stay away!

TODD: Don't be afraid.

EMMA: Stay where you are!

TODD: I'm your brother.

EMMA: I don't have a brother!

TODD: I've been away a long time.

EMMA: My stomach hurts.

TODD: But I'm back.

EMMA: My skin is too tight.

TODD: What's wrong with you?

EMMA: I don't have any brothers or sisters!

TODD: Look at me Emma!

EMMA: My father'll be home soon! If you touch me, he'll kill you!

TODD: Look at me!

EMMA: He's the chief of police! He's a Nazi! He'll kill you!

TODD: (*Grabbing her.*) Think!

EMMA: Let me go!

TODD: Remember growing up!

EMMA: You're hurting me!

TODD: We played games!

EMMA: Oh, God! You're going to rape me, aren't you! GOD! DADDY! GOD! HELP ME!

TODD: Think! (*She breaks free.*) Emma!?

EMMA: (*Threatening him with a letter opener.*) I don't know who you are, but get out of here or I'll kill you myself! I WILL!

TODD: I just needed a place to stay— (*Grace rushes on.*)

GRACE: Emma! What on earth's going— (*She sees Todd.*) Todd?

TODD: Mother. (*Grace and Todd embrace.*)

EMMA: (*To herself.*) There's something wrong with me. There's something very wrong.

GRACE: Let me look at you!

TODD: How are you, Mother?

GRACE: Emma, why didn't you tell me your brother—

EMMA: I don't have a brother!!

TODD: I'm home, Mother.

EMMA: Who is this person?

GRACE: She forgets things.

EMMA: I'd remember a brother.

GRACE: Well, you'd think so — Todd, let me look at you.

EMMA: What's going on here?

GRACE: Oh, think, Emma. You remember Todd. Think! He went away five years ago to study sculpting?

EMMA: I don't think so.

GRACE: Think back. When you were twelve we went to Washington? We had a picnic. We sat on the lawn and ate sandwiches and grapes. You got amebic dysentery.

EMMA: Who did?

TODD: When you were ten we all went to London, for Christmas.

GRACE: We ate lard and salty beans.

TODD: We walked the bridge in the cold dank mist.

EMMA: I don't know what anyone's talking about.

GRACE: She represses.

TODD: She's lucky.

GRACE: What an ironic remark. Isn't your brother ironic?

EMMA: Who?

GRACE: Skip it — You look thin. Are you eating?

TODD: You mean right now?

GRACE: I meant in general.

TODD: Oh.

GRACE: It's wonderful to see you — How long can you stay — Your father'll be thrilled!

TODD: He will?

GRACE: He'll be home soon. He's at the bank.

TODD: On a Sunday?

GRACE: Is it Sunday?

EMMA: (*Out.*) Who are these people?

GRACE: I was just saying to Nina Triten how I wish you'd come home for a visit. I was beginning to think you didn't like us. And now, here you are! You're a man! A grown up! Do I look different? I've just lost five pounds. I eat lemon zest and bib lettuce! Prisoners on death row eat better than I! — I've stopped smoking. That was three years ago. When Bunny Witton died of emphysema, I took it for a sign — You look well. Your clothes don't fit and I must admit they're dirty.

TODD: They're comfortable.

GRACE: We'll get you some new clothes. We'll go shopping first thing in the morning. Remember how we used to go shopping? You'll need a blazer. I saw a beautiful Byblos at Plage Tahiti — Where are my manners!? You must be starved! How did you get here? Would you like a drink?

TODD: No thank you.

EMMA: I would. (*Grace rings bell.*)

GRACE: Be honest. I look older, don't I? I shouldn't. I had my eyes done last August, but one's tighter than the other and now everyone thinks I'm winking at them all the time — I know! We'll have a party! How long can you stay?

TODD: I don't think that's —

GRACE: It's decided! I have decided. You'll be the guest of honor!

TODD: I have AIDS.

GRACE: (*After a moment.*) We'll have a buffet, that'll be nice. You give me a list of what you'd like. Or we could barbecue. That'd be sweet. I don't have any idea what you like anymore.

TODD: I have AIDS. I need a bed and a place to live. I have AIDS.

GRACE: (*Falling apart, plowing ahead.*) Your father can string up those paper lanterns. The one's we used at your sister's sweet sixteen. We still have them I think. I think they're in the attic. We packed them away. I think , with the Christmas ornaments.

TODD: I need a pillow and some peace and quiet.

EMMA: Who are you?

GRACE: We'll serve champagne or punch, or something to drink.

TODD: I have —

GRACE: (*Her despair now shows.*) And the Beekmans'll come! Essie was always fond of you. She's married now. Gotten fat. Don't be shocked when you see her.

TODD: I said —

GRACE: I don't think she's happy really. She married a nice enough man. Very attractive. In real estate.

TODD: I have AIDS.

GRACE: I think he beats hero.

Todd: I have AIDS.

GRACE: And the Plimptons.

TODD: Listen to me.

GRACE: (*Rather frenzied now.*) And the Weathertons — maybe we should cater! I don't know — I love planning a party! I feel I'm really in my element when I'm planning a party! We'll have music on the terrace! I'm most alive when planning a party! You'll see, Todd, it'll be wonderful! It'll be beautiful! You're going to love it! You're just going to love it!

TODD: I have AIDS. (*There is a blackout.*)

VLADIVOSTOK BLUES

Jocelyn Beard

2 Men, 1 Woman
  Stu Bernstein (30s), a talent manager; the Inspector (40–50); a tired
  Russian policeman; and Lena (20s), the inspector's pert assistant.

Scene: A police station in Vladivostok

Stu's biggest client is Sophia La Cruz, the star of "Forever Angelina," a
Mexican soap opera. At Stu's insistence, Sophia has agreed to a ten-
city personal appearance tour of Russia, where "Forever Angelina" is
the number one show. On the last night of the tour, Sophia is kidnapped by a crazed fan. Here, the desperate Stu does his best to moti-
vate the local authorities.

○   ○   ○

*(Lights up on police station. Stu Bernstein paces nervously
across the floor, chewing on a cigarette that he will never light.
Stu is dressed stylishly and with great expense. Armani, Armani,
Armani. [The three A's of fashion.] He wears a small gold hoop
earring in his ear. The Inspector enters. He is a tired looking
man carrying an enormous stack of papers.)*

STU: Jesus Christ! It took you long enough! Did you find it?

INSPECTOR: *(Dropping the papers on his desk with a thud.)* It must
  be in here somewhere.

STU: Oh for… listen, Inspector, shouldn't you be putting some men
  on this? You know, sending them out *(Gestures dramatically.)*
  there… to find her?

INSPECTOR: Men?

STU: *(Exasperated.)* You know… your officers! Police… people!
  Sophia isn't in that pile of paper! She's out *(Gestures again.)*
  there!!

INSPECTOR: So, you know where she is!

STU: What? No! I don't know where Sophia is! I only know where
  she isn't, which is right here in this room where nothing is

being done to find her! *(The door to the Inspector's office bursts open and Lena enters. She is an attractive young woman in uniform carrying a tray with a tea service which she places on the desk.)*

INSPECTOR: Ahhh, tea.

STU: *(To Lena.)* Did you make those calls?

LENA: Yes, Mr. Bernstein. *(Turns to leave.)*

STU: Wait a minute! *(Runs in between Lena and the door.)* And…?

LENA: And?

STU: The calls…?

LENA: The calls…?

STU: Did you get through? Did you talk to anyone at the embassy?

LENA: *(Smiling.)* Oh, yes!

STU: And…?

LENA: And…? Oh, yes! I spoke with the most delightful man! Some kind of secretary I believe he said he was… Octavio, yes I believe that he said his name was Octavio. Very charming. Said to look him up the next time I'm in Moscow. *(The Inspector has busied himself with pouring himself a cup of tea. He now sits in his chair and sips it happily, his back to the papers.)*

STU: *(Barely containing his exasperation, through clenched teeth.)* What else did he say?

LENA: *(Thinking.)* Nothing.

STU: Nothing????

LENA: *(Thinking harder.)* No, that was it.

STU: Okay, let me get this straight. You phoned the Mexican Embassy in Moscow and informed a secretary named Octavio—a charming and delightful man—that the most famous citizen of his country has just been kidnapped at gun point right here in Vladivostok, and all he had to say was "Look me up the next time you're in town"?!?!

LENA: Oh my!

STU: What? What does that mean, oh my?

LENA: Well, you see, I never told him.

STU: Never told him what?

LENA: About Angelina… I mean, Sophia.

STU: *(Thundering.)* YOU NEVER TOLD HIM?????

LENA: Well, you see, I called and asked to speak with the Ambassador who, as it turns out, is at the symphony, so when I wasn't able to speak with the Ambassador, I asked Octavio if I could leave a message for him to call here as soon as he can... and then we just started chatting...

STU: *(Nearly hysterical.)* Chatting? You were chatting?

LENA: Yes, Mr. Bernstein. Chatting.

STU: And it never once occurred to you to tell this Octavio about Sophia?

LENA: Well, I thought it might be a secret.

STU: A secret?

LENA: *(Defensively.)* Yes, Mr. Bernstein, a secret. You Americans are always keeping secrets! Every American I've ever met was keeping some big secret or another.

STU: Okay, okay. Calm down. *(Fumbling in his pockets and finding a bottle of pills. He struggles with the cap and then swallows a handful.)* Okay... okay. *(Taking a deep breath and letting it out.)* Ohmm... ohmmmm... ohmmm mane padne ohmmmmmm. *(Another deep breath.)* Okay. *(Turns his attention back to Lena.)* Here we go. Miss...?

LENA: Officer?

STU: Right. Officer...?

LENA: Oh, please, call me Lena.

STU: Why, thank you, Lena. Lena.

LENA: Yes?

STU: I want you to go back to your desk and get Octavio back on the line.

LENA: Yes?

STU: I want you to get him back on the line and I want you to tell him that Sophia La Cruz, the star of "Forever Angelina," the number one rated soap opera worldwide, has been kidnapped.

LENA: *(Making a note on a notepad.)* Kidnapped.

STU: That's right, Lena. Tell Octavio that Sophia La Cruz, the most loved and admired woman in Mexico and a personal favorite of the president—who never misses an episode—has been kidnapped.

LENA: *(Still writing.)* Kidnapped.

STU: Yes, kidnapped. You tell that charming Octavio that Sophia La Cruz, a woman with more international clout than Henry Kissinger, whose face appears every day on television sets from here to kingdomfuckingcome, who is adored by miserable people everywhere, has been KIDNAPPED right here in your little shithole—the same shithole, I might add, that wasn't on our original itinerary but whose mayor begged, yes begged me to include on the tour.

LENA: *(Scribbling frantically.)* ...kidnapped...shithole...

STU: And then you tell this Octavio that in the *(Checks watch.)* five hours that have passed since Sophia was carried kicking and screaming from that wretched excuse of a dressing room by some lunatic waving a gun, that in those five long hours you—the police—have done nothing, nada, zilch, *(Russian.)* to find her.

LENA: *(Writing.)* ...zilch to find her.

STU: Good. Then you tell Octavio to get in his car and drive to the goddamn symphony and get the Ambassador and bring him back to the Embassy, because in about *(Checks watch again.)* oh, five more hours, when I have to inform Sophia's husband, agent and producer that she's been kidnapped, he's going to have an international incident on his hands.

LENA: *(Writing.)* International incident...

STU: That's right, an international incident. So you tell Octavio that we've got about five hours before I have to make the call that will end his career. Five hours to find Sophia. Five hours before the end of the world as we know it.

LENA: *(Writing.)* Five hours... end of world.

STU: Any questions?

LENA: *(Looking up with a smile.)* No, I've got it!

STU: So...?

LENA: Yes?

STU: So, go! Make the call!

LENA: I'm on it, Mr. Bernstein! *(Lena exits crisply. Stu seems to collapse in on himself. He turns back to the Inspector.)*

STU: Okay. So, Inspector, what are you doing to find... *(A loud snore from the Inspector cuts him off. Stu stares incredulously at the sleeping man and then collapses onto a chair. Swallowing more pills.)* Ohmmmm! Ohmmmmm. Ohmmmm mane padne ohmmmm... *(Lights out on police station.)*

THE VOYEUR AND THE WIDOW

Le Wilhelm

1 Man, 1 Woman
Elgin (16–20) a voyeur, and Edwina (20s) a widow.

Scene: A porch at twilight

Here, two acquaintances share a cigarette and a little insight on a warm evening.

○   ○   ○

EDWINA: Elgin, what are you doing out here? *(Edwina is a little bit older than Elgin. She is in her early to mid-twenties.)*

ELGIN: *(Startled.)* Geez!

EDWINA: I didn't mean to startle you.

ELGIN: What's wrong with you?

EDWINA: Nothing.

ELGIN: What do you mean sneaking up on someone like that?

EDWINA: I didn't sneak up on you.

ELGIN: I sure didn't see you coming.

EDWINA: That's 'cause you were busy with that cigarette.

ELGIN: So.

EDWINA: I know your daddy don't believe in cigarette smoking.

ELGIN: I do what I like.

EDWINA: You don't need to be hiding it from me. I don't care how many cigarettes you smoke. *(He takes the cigarette and lights it. She looks at him and smiles.)* Elgin, if you were a little older, or if you were a gentleman, you'd know the correct procedure at this time is to offer a lady a smoke.

ELGIN: Huh?

EDWINA: *(Exasperated.)* Give me a cigarette, Elgin!

ELGIN: Geez.

EDWINA: Don't be such a tightwad.

ELGIN: I only got two, Edwina.

EDWINA: After you give me one, you'll only have one, and that should be enough to get you through the night.

ELGIN: I guess.

EDWINA: What'd you do, steal these?

ELGIN: Huh?

EDWINA: You heard me!! Don't say "huh" when you hear what someone said.

ELGIN: Why are you so all fired mean today?

EDWINA: I know you stole these cigarettes, 'cause if you'd gone in the store and bought 'em, then Elsie would have called your daddy and told him that you were buying cigarettes from her at the store.

ELGIN: That's the truth. You can't do nothing around this town without everyone knowing your business. I can't wait, in a couple of years I'm getting out of here.

EDWINA: You'll be going in the army.

ELGIN: Probably. And if'n I do, it'll be the last this town sees of me.

EDWINA: I pretty well know how you feel. People around here are just low-down. That's what they are, just low-down hypocrites! I just have a good notion to go get a bunch of rocks and break the windows in this store.

ELGIN: What did they do to you?

EDWINA: Nothing! I'm just mad. I'm as mad as a nest of hornets in a hailstorm.

ELGIN: How come?

EDWINA: Female things.

ELGIN: Oh.

EDWINA: You wouldn't understand.

ELGIN: You find out Ray Dean's been sparking Dorothy Sue behind your back?

EDWINA: *(Aghast.)* Who told you that?

ELGIN: Everyone knows that.

EDWINA: Wonderful.

ELGIN: You didn't have any idea?

EDWINA: No.

ELGIN: I just figured you knew, 'cause everyone else did.

EDWINA: Oh just shut your trap.

ELGIN: It ain't my fault.

EDWINA: I'll just go on and get this over to Mrs. Solomon's house.

ELGIN: What are you going over to her house for?

EDWINA: She called Momma asking her if she had any paint sitting around the house that she might have. Course Momma said sure, she had some red enamel that she'd never use and that I'd be more than glad to bring it over.

ELGIN: What's Mrs. Solomon painting?

EDWINA: Birds.

ELGIN: What?

EDWINA: She had someone saw her a bunch of wood in the shape of birds, and she's going to paint them and put them on her fenceposts, I guess, you know like how old people do. I guess they're going to be red birds.

ELGIN: What if you'd had some other color of paint. If the paint would have been black, would she have painted them black and had crows?

EDWINA: I don't know, Elgin. I don't care!! I just get sick and tired of Momma volunteering me for everything that comes up in this little hick town. She's got me running all over the country-side delivering and picking up things all the time.

ELGIN: You ain't got nothing better to do, do you?

EDWINA: Elgin, do you not realize that less than two years ago, I lost my young husband in that awful war.

ELGIN: I know that.

EDWINA: I loved Jim Bob with all my heart, and today I find out my boyfriend of six months is running around behind my back with Dorothy Sue Call, who is a married woman and whose husband Leonard is fighting the selfsame war in which my husband died.

ELGIN: I know all that!

EDWINA: Oh, it's not senses talking to you.

ELGIN: What are you trying to say, Edwina?

EDWINA: I'm trying to say that my life ain't easy. I'm trying to say that I've had me a real bad day, and I think you could just be the least bit sympathetic to my plight.

ELGIN: Could I ask something, Edwina?

EDWINA: What?

ELGIN: Are you going to smoke that cigarette or are you going to stand there and wave it around like it's some demented fly that can't make up its mind where to land?

EDWINA: I'd smoke it if someone would light it for me, since I'm obviously not in the possession of any matches.

ELGIN: All you have to do is ask, Edwina.

EDWINA: Oh! I'm so glad I've got you to explain the social graces to me, Elgin. May I have a light?

ELGIN: Sure. *(Lights the cigarette.)* Sit down. Take a load off, Edwina.

EDWINA: *(Looks at him like he's crazy.)* Thanks. *(After a moment.)*

ELGIN: You shouldn't be too mad at Ray Dean!

EDWINA: I'll be the judge of that.

ELGIN: He was sparking Dorothy Sue afore he even started going out with you.

EDWINA: You don't know what you're talking about.

ELGIN: Yes, I do. I seen him and her parked up at Barrel Springs over a year ago.

EDWINA: Are you sure?

ELGIN: I'm sure.

EDWINA: Maybe they's just talking.

ELGIN: Maybe. But they were in the back seat of his Ford.

EDWINA: Still, that doesn't mean there was anything illicit going on.

ELGIN: Her feet were hanging out the window.

EDWINA: Oh.

ELGIN: They were making a lot of noise, but they weren't saying any words. Least none that I understood.

EDWINA: I get the picture, Elgin.

ELGIN: You'd be surprised the people who end up parked at Barrel Springs.

EDWINA: Right now nothing would surprise me!

ELGIN: Yes sir, lots of folks end up at Barrel Springs.

EDWINA: What are you doing up there all the time, Elgin?

ELGIN: I go up there and watch.

EDWINA: That's disgusting.

ELGIN: I've been doing it since I was ten years old. Hide up there in the rocks and wait for someone to show up. Most nights they do.

EDWINA: That sounds like you might be sick, Elgin.

ELGIN: What are you saying?

EDWINA: Like you might be one of them voyeur people.

ELGIN: What's that?

EDWINA: Like a Peeping Tom. Someone who enjoys watching other people do… things. You know.

ELGIN: I don't enjoy it. I do it for my education.

EDWINA: I see. *(Pause.)* No, I don't.

ELGIN: You know my father.

EDWINA: Yeah.

ELGIN: Well, I decided when I was real young that what I wanted to be was a really good lovemaker. But I also found myself in quite a strange situation. Because I couldn't go to my father and have him tell me things. 'Sides I'm not sure he knows how to be a good lovemaker.

EDWINA: Probably not.

ELGIN: So, I figured that the only way I could learn is if I watched and listened to people.

EDWINA: And so you go up to Barrel Springs and hide and listen and watch…

ELGIN: Yes, ma'am. I do.

EDWINA: I think that's disgusting, Elgin.

ELGIN: It may be, but I aim to have my education. I've seen you up there, Edwina.

EDWINA: Elgin!!

ELGIN: Nothing to be embarrassed about. I saw you up there with Jim Bob.

EDWINA: Jim Bob and I only parked up at Barrel Springs one time.

ELGIN: Only saw the two of you up there once.

EDWINA: That was a special night.

ELGIN: *(Smiling.)* Yes, ma'am.

EDWINA: That was the night he asked me to be his wife.

ELGIN: And it sure made you happy.

EDWINA: *(Unashamed.)* Yes, it did.

ELGIN: I've seen you up there with Ray Dean.

EDWINA: I don't want to hear about Ray Dean right now.

ELGIN: You don't get in the back seat with him, do you?

EDWINA: No, I don't. I know a lot about Ray Dean, and one thing I know is when a woman crawls in the back seat with him, it won't be six months before she's gone and he's with another.

ELGIN: And you figure the only way to keep him is not to go all the way with him?

EDWINA: That's right.

ELGIN: Would you like another cigarette, Edwina?

EDWINA: I thought you said you only had one left?

ELGIN: *(Smiles.)* I lied. *(Edwina takes the cigarette. Immediately he lights it for her.)* See. I learn fast.

The Best
Women's Scenes
of 1994

CARELESS LOVE

Len Jenkin

2 Women

Marie (20s) a young poet/actress, and the Wife (30s) a disturbed woman holding her hostage.

Scene: Geneva

Marie has been taken hostage by a psychotic plastic surgeon who has brought her to his home in Geneva. Here, Marie has an interesting encounter with the doctor's unbalanced wife.

○ ○ ○

MARIE: *(Urgent whisper.)* Where am I? *(Siren and carousel end abruptly. Silence. A cuckoo clock chimes.)*

WIFE: You're in Geneva—Switzerland. To be more specific, you're standing by a window in my living room. You're Marie, aren't you? The hostage? My husband told me everything about you. He's gone out to market whatever psychoactive garbage was in the leather case. Spanish leather, by the way.

MARIE: From Cordoba, probably.

WIFE: How did you know?

MARIE: Just a feeling.

WIFE: In any case, he's left you with me. *(The surgeon's wife goes over to a table—coffee pot, snacks.)*

WIFE: Would you like some *smurrbrot?*

MARIE: Just coffee, please. Uh, how do you like your husband's new face?

WIFE: Cheap. He looks like an ad for a cut-rate men's shop. But it doesn't matter. He's the same man. Impossible. I tell him to stop this cops-and-robbers routine, and he says we're broke, we need the money. He says he owes Lorenzo—that demented little bastard. I run an overpriced art gallery here, and another one in Munich. We're quite wealthy, actually. My husband's insane.

MARIE: *(Under her breath.)* I noticed…

WIFE: Did he mention Rapunzel?

MARIE: Yes.

WIFE: And the flames, leaping up her golden hair?

MARIE: Yes.

WIFE: And our poor son, burnt to a black cinder.

MARIE: Yes. I'm so…

WIFE: We never had a son. We can't have children. He's sterile, actually. Not that I mind. His fairy tale. It gives him permission to behave very badly. As badly as Lorenzo, with his celestial bed, his Egyptian cigarettes, that nasty monkey Tomas, who shits on the furniture—his insane tips on the Tokyo stock market… Do you know what I believe? Do you?

MARIE: No. How could I know what…

WIFE: My husband and Lorenzo are actually… *(Laughs.)* It's none of your business, you nosy, prying bitch.

MARIE: Hey, I didn't even…

WIFE: I do have my own theory as to why young people like yourself are in so much pain—so much uncertainty about their… orientation. It's simple actually. Everything's fucked, darling. Ugly, crooked, and crazy.

MARIE: You're wrong. Our life can *seem* stupid and unhappy, but there's always something fine and brave about it at the same time. I know that, under all the crap, we're all quite beautiful and pure inside. Your husband, and Bobby, and me. You too.

WIFE: Am I beautiful and pure inside?

MARIE: Yes.

WIFE: Think what you like. I always do. It doesn't matter anyway. You want love, Marie—and honesty, and peace—and a little touch of God's grace to brighten it all. You'll never have any of it. The true life of men and women beats in darkness and blood. We begin in a pointless convulsion of desire. We end staring up into the fluorescents, longing for the dumb mouth of the grave. Do as I do, Little Marie. Make the best of this bad dream. Say your prayers. Kneel. Kneel, dammit. *(The surgeon's wife twists Marie's arm, pressing her down. Marie kneels. The surgeon's wife kneels alongside her, runs a hand gently over her hair.)*

WIFE: Repeat after me. Now I lay me down to sleep…

MARIE: Now I lay me down to sleep

WIFE: I pray the Lord my soul to keep

MARIE: I pray the Lord my soul to keep.

WIFE: If I die before I wake…

MARIE: If I die before I wake…

WIFE: I pray the Lord my soul to take.

MARIE: I pray the Lord my soul to take. *(The surgeon's wife kisses Marie on the lips. Then she rises, and walks away.)*

WIFE: I'd like to take you to dinner tonight. At La Perle du Lac, by the waterside on the Rue des Singes. The food is quite nice. Then we can have a nightcap at The Inn of the Sun, where the most wonderful things can happen…

MARIE: No, thanks.

WIFE: More coffee? You're free to leave, by the way. We don't need you anymore. He thinks we do, but I hate hostages. Besides, I'm jealous. I'll do my best to distract him when he finds out you're gone. *(The Wife produces a key.)* The key to his air-mobile. Follow me. *(The airmobile appears, and the Surgeon's Wife hands Marie the key.)* Just get right in. *(The Wife shoves Marie into the vehicle, and slams the door.)* There! Nice and cozy. My love to Bobby.

MARIE: You don't even know Bobby. Besides, he's dead.

WIFE: Start the engine, you little fool.

MARIE: I don't know if I can drive this…

WIFE: It drives itself. Trust me. *(Marie starts up the mighty airmobile. It idles. The Wife is suddenly holding a videocassette.)*

WIFE: Take this.

MARIE: A videocassette?

WIFE: There's a player in the dash.

MARIE: You rented me a movie?

WIFE: Screen it on your way home. *(Police sirens in the distance, approaching. The Surgeon's Wife begins to walk away.)*

MARIE: *(Calling after her.)* How do I get home? And that plastic surgeon still has Bobby's face! You people will never get away with…

WIFE: *(Turning back to Marie.)* Step on it, darling. That airmobile is being hunted by the Swiss police. They're merciless to foreigners. *(Police sirens, louder, closer.)* Go! Go! *(A great roar, and the airmobile takes off.)* Call me sometime.

THE CONFIRMATION

Kier Peters

2 Women
 Grandma (88) a cantankerous old woman, and Mother (30–40) a woman living in a state of denial.

Scene: Here and Now

Grandma's memory seems a bit spotty, as evidenced by the following conversation which takes place as Mother prepares for the old woman's eighty-eighth birthday.

O   O   O

(In the middle of a yard stands a woman with a large straw garden hat. She points at Grandma, sitting on a couch.)

MOTHER: Now sit down there very nicely and be out of the way!

GRANDMA: What?

MOTHER: Sit down very nice.

GRANDMA: *(Looking about.)* Where is the house?

MOTHER: *(Busying herself.)* We will build one around you and me one day.

GRANDMA: Who?

MOTHER: The man whom I may marry then.

GRANDMA: Who?

MOTHER: You'll know him when he comes.

GRANDMA: I will?

MOTHER: And everyone will be happy in the end. *(Taking a pie out of the stove.)* As soon as it cools down I'll cut you a slice.

GRANDMA: What kind?

MOTHER: You know I've forgotten what I put in it.

GRANDMA: Because I don't like cherry or apricot.

MOTHER: I don't think it's cherry and I doubt I've made apricot since it's something I've never done.

GRANDMA: And I don't like apple nor blueberry nor rhubarb, mince, banana, raisin, or chocolate.

MOTHER: Gee I don't know what to say it might be one of those it just might.

GRANDMA: Nor lemon nor lime nor peach. I completely hate peach.

MOTHER: Well Grandma what do you like?

GRANDMA: *(Screwing up her face.)* I forgot.

MOTHER: *(Putting down the pie.)* I'm not going to serve it then besides it wasn't really a pie. It's a cake.

GRANDMA: I like cake.

MOTHER: I guess you would with almost ninety candles to blow out.

GRANDMA: Is it my birthday?

MOTHER: You know I don't remember. When were you born?

GRANDMA: Before the War.

MOTHER: Which war?

GRANDMA: Have there been more?

MOTHER: Plenty yes. You must recall Herman your husband died in the first and his brother's son in the second one. And his son Mark died in Korea and his son Dick died in Laos.

GRANDMA: What was he doing in Laos?

MOTHER: Now that's something we never found out.

GRANDMA: Where is it?

MOTHER: One of those jungles I think.

GRANDMA: Who'd have thought.

MOTHER: Who would? I guess the military might. Their job is to think of strange places for men to die in.

GRANDMA: What was your name again?

MOTHER: Now Grandma sit down very nice.

GRANDMA: I need to stand. I need to walk about.

MOTHER: O dear that you can't.

GRANDMA: Can't what?

MOTHER: Remember you fell and broke your whole hip one night.

GRANDMA: Never did such a thing in my life.

MOTHER: Oh but you did! And the doctors said it was doubtful you would ever walk again they did.

GRANDMA: *(Attempting to rise.)* Pooh on them!

MOTHER: Now Grandma what a way to talk!

GRANDMA: *(Sitting down again.)* I'll talk as I walk and I'll do both just as I please thank you.

MOTHER: You've no one to thank but yourself. Marching around in the dark of night.

GRANDMA: I had to pee.

MOTHER: If this goes on I'm going to have to put a patch of tape across your mouth. Besides they found you by your own front door.

GRANDMA: I wanted to whizz.

MOTHER: *(Skeptical.)* Now you're just being difficult. You've had plumbing for forty years or more.

GRANDMA: Can't get used to it.

MOTHER: Well you don't have to worry anymore at least not until I meet Mr. Right.

GRANDMA: At your age you're not going to meet anyone.

MOTHER: Now Grandma that hurts where it hurts plunk through the heart. And remember you met Mr. Billingslea at fifty-three?

GRANDMA: Who?

MOTHER: Your third husband Mr. Billingslea.

GRANDMA: He was black.

MOTHER: *(Laughing.)* Now what made you think that? He was white as that lily plant with hands just as pale to match.

GRANDMA: He was a nigra.

MOTHER: Well if that was so he certainly fooled me and everyone else and you, if I know you as I do who is terrified of colored men, Islamic women, and Indian children who talk too fast, wouldn't have been marrying one of them!

GRANDMA: I'll marry anyone I like.

MOTHER: And I will too as long as he builds us a house around all the comforts we've collected for ourselves.

GRANDMA: The sun's too bright.

MOTHER: It's nearly noon Grandma love. Here take out your umbrella *(Putting an umbrella into her mother's hand)*.

GRANDMA: I don't remember this.

MOTHER: Well you don't remember anything anymore much it's true.

GRANDMA: I remember I don't like you.

MOTHER: You never did. Always talking Harry Harry Harry even when we were growing up, never a word of praise to Mary or me or poor poor Blanche.

GRANDMA: I liked Blanche, I bet I did 'cause I like her name still yet today.

MOTHER: Well you certainly had a funny way of showing it keeping her locked away from all the rest.

GRANDMA: Who?

MOTHER: Poor Poor Blanche.

GRANDMA: I locked her away from… you and Mary and Harry and everyone else you say I knew? I wanted her to grow up better.

MOTHER: But to teach her nothing but Norwegian really! She couldn't even communicate with us.

GRANDMA: (Smiling.) I did that?

MOTHER: Yes you certainly did, you wouldn't let her communicate with anyone else.

GRANDMA: And did she learn the formal tense?

MOTHER: How would I know not knowing a single word of it. I just remember poor poor Blanche whom they took away one day when they found out what you did.

GRANDMA: Who? Who found out?

MOTHER: The authorities. The school board and the social worker and then that dreadful nurse.

GRANDMA: Pooh on the nurse!

MOTHER: Well there I agree taking away Mary who was as perfectly normal as you and me all because Blanche was treated so specially.

GRANDMA: What happened to that Mary then?

MOTHER: Now Grandma you can't pretend to have forgotten that!

GRANDMA: I remember I guess she ran away and had to get married and became a nymphomaniac.

MOTHER: What an imagination you've got!

GRANDMA: That's what I recall.

MOTHER: She was taken by a Catholic family who converted her quick.

GRANDMA: Converted her from what?

MOTHER: From Protestantism surely! At least that's what I always thought! We went to Public High.

GRANDMA: Was there a Catholic one?

MOTHER: Maybe not.

GRANDMA: So?

MOTHER: Well anyway Mary became one and then became a nun.

GRANDMA: I was a nun.

MOTHER: What?

GRANDMA: Before I got married.

MOTHER: Now Grandma you know you were not!

GRANDMA: Was so! I remember that much!

MOTHER: All right if you say so but I was brought up Protestant.

GRANDMA: By who?

MOTHER: By Daddy and you.

GRANDMA: Now I remember Harry and I think I can remember Blanche and I can even once in while imagine I had a daughter Mary but I certainly don't remember a thing about Protestantism!

MOTHER: Are you doubting my word I've had just about enough. *(Calling.)* Mary come out! Come out!

FIVE WOMEN WEARING THE SAME DRESS

Alan Ball

2 Women

Trisha and Georgeanne (30s), two old friends acting as bridesmaids at a wedding.

Scene: A wedding reception

Trisha, Georgreanne, and Tracy have been friends for many years. When Trisha and Georgeanne find themselves acting as bridesmaids at Tracy's wedding, they take a break from the festivities to reminisce about their college days.

O   O   O

GEORGEANNE: All right. Enough about me, more about my *dress*. Can you believe Tracy made us wear these things?

TRISHA: Yes.

GEORGEANNE: Of course, I can't believe she asked me to be in her wedding—

TRISHA: I can't believe you accepted.

GEORGEANNE: Well, I didn't have any choice, Trisha. What was I supposed to say? Tracy, I don't think I can be in your wedding, because you remember when I had that nervous breakdown my junior year of college? That was because your boyfriend knocked me up and I had to have an abortion all by myself while he was taking you to the Kappa Sig Luau, and things have been just a little, well, *strained* between you and me ever since.

TRISHA: Have you ever talked to her about it?

GEORGEANNE: Oh. No, neither one of us has ever mentioned it. *(Looking out window.)* And now here she is, getting married to Scott McClure, the biggest piece of wet toast I ever saw in my life. 'Course I married Chuck Darby, the *second* biggest piece of wet toast I ever saw, because I thought I wanted some *stability*.

And there's Tommy Valentine, getting ready to rip that little bitch's backless linen dress off of her scrawny little body and fuck her brains out. God, I wish I was her.

TRISHA: *(Exasperated.)* Oh, please. You do not.

GEORGEANNE: Oh, yes I do. I am wearing over a hundred dollars worth of extremely uncomfortable lingerie from Victoria's Secret that I bought specifically for him to rip off of *me.*

TRISHA: *(Staring at her.)* You honestly thought you were going to sleep with Tommy Valentine today?

GEORGEANNE: Well. Yeah, I mean, why not? Remember page sixty-seven of *The Godfather?*

TRISHA: I think your memories of him might be just a little rosy, I mean it has been almost, what, ten years?

GEORGEANNE: Three months.

TRISHA: Excuse me? *(Georgeanne nods guiltily.)* Georgeanne, you better spill your guts to me right now.

GEORGEANNE: I ran into him at this sleazy bar that only plays fifties and sixties music? I hate those places but at least I'm not the oldest one there. He seemed really happy to see me, and then we started flirting, but it wasn't gross, it was real sweet— *Trisha laughs.)* I'm serious, it was.

TRISHA: I'm so sure.

GEORGEANNE: You weren't there!

TRISHA: I've been there. So then what happened?

GEORGEANNE: Well, we closed the bar, and he asked me if I wanted to go somewhere where we could be alone. I said, look, this is not a good idea, I'm married, I have a little boy. And once I said that? It's like I didn't have to worry about it. I had said it, so it was out of the way. And I just went nuts, we ended up doing it in the parking lot, on the concrete, right behind a Dempsey Dumpster. *(Pause.)*

TRISHA: *(Impressed.)* Wow. That's pretty good.

GEORGEANNE: Trisha, it was the best sex I ever had in my entire life. I will never, ever be able to smell garbage again without thinking about it. So my memories of Tommy are pretty recent and pretty accurate, I think.

TRISHA: Yeah, but Georgeanne. Did he call you after that?

GEORGEANNE: No.

TRISHA: Okay, so here's this guy who totally bagged out on his responsibility to you, left you to go through an abortion all by yourself. Ten years later, he fucks you in a parking lot and then he ignores you. And you still want him.

GEORGEANNE: I can't help it. I love him.

TRISHA: That's not love, that's addiction.

GEORGEANNE: Well, I'm sorry, but I hadn't had sex in over a year. And I wouldn't mind making a habit of it.

TRISHA: What? *(Pause.)*

GEORGEANNE: Chuck and I don't even sleep in the same bed anymore. He sleeps in the guest room.

TRISHA: Why?

GEORGEANNE: I don't know.

TRISHA: You have some idea. You have to.

GEORGEANNE: He doesn't talk to me, Trisha. It's like I'm not even there. I told Chuck about Tommy, the next day. He just looked at me with this fish face, and then he said, "You don't have to tell me everything you do." *(She starts to cry.)*

TRISHA: *(Irritated.)* Georgeanne!

GEORGEANNE: What can I do?

TRISHA: *Make* Chuck talk to you. Make him go to a counselor.

GEORGEANNE: No.

TRISHA: Do you want to save your marriage?

GEORGEANNE: No! I *don't!* I never should have married him in the first place, just like you said. I don't love him. I don't even like him! *(Suddenly, the door opens and Mindy enters. She is an attractive, slender woman in her mid to late thirties. She is dressed exactly like the others.)*

FLOATING RHODA AND THE GLUE MAN

Eve Ensler

2 Women
Rhoda (30s), a woman searching for love, and Terrace (30s), her best friend.

Scene: Here and Now

Here, two friends share banter and comfort following a workout.

○   ○   ○

RHODA: No, he's good. You can tell he's good.

TERRACE: The guy is good. Good like sweet. Good like boring. Good like bread dough?

RHODA: Good like "wouldn't fuck around." Good like political.

TERRACE: Like Greenpeace dolphin protector, like A.C.L.U. lawyer, good like that.

RHODA: Forget good. Good is a moron word. Good is reactionary. Good is a first lady kind of word. It's a plastered smile kind of word. Good was the wrong word. Good is a ruined word. Like so many words. Happiness, truth, recovery, holocaust, . . . You cannot use these words. Particularly with you.

TERRACE: He's Jewish Rhoda?

RHODA: No, he's thin Terrace okay? And clear.

TERRACE: Clear? Like weather? Like visionary, like . . .

RHODA: Terrace, you're asking questions again. I thought you were working with your therapist to stop asking questions.

TERRACE: Oh God. You're right. It's a slip. I'm having a question slip. It's compulsive you know? My therapist said I ask a lot of questions because I am terrified of the chaos and mess. Questions, she said, give me an illusionary sense of order and control.

RHODA: Why not get a machine gun? It doesn't require so much energy and it's only momentarily annoying.

TERRACE: Funny Rhoda.

RHODA: It's one blind date Terrace. I don't know this guy. There were angels in his photographs. He was nervous and available.

TERRACE: Are you still with that carnivores man?

RHODA: You mean Coyote?

TERRACE: Who has a name like that?

RHODA: He's really different than you think. He's definitely going somewhere.

TERRACE: Prison Rhoda?

RHODA: You never like my men.

TERRACE: You don't either Rhoda.

RHODA: That's true Terrace. (*They both collapse from the exercises. Rhoda's stand-in continues, showing off.*)

RHODA: Do my arm the way you do Terrace.

TERRACE: Rhoda, I'm exhausted.

RHODA: Please Terrace. I think I only work out so you'll do my arm like that. (*Terrace begins to tickle Rhoda's arm. Rhoda playfully moans, deeply enjoying it. This encourages Terrace to get into it.*)

RHODA: I told him you had great breasts.

TERRACE: Who? Coyote?

RHODA: No, the guy.

TERRACE: You told him about my breasts.

RHODA: You know I love your breasts. I really admire them. Because they're real, because they're practical and ripe, because they stay up in lycra without a bra.

TERRACE: I think it's weird.

RHODA: What?

TERRACE: That you told a strange guy about my breasts.

RHODA: I didn't tell him "about" your breasts. I just told him you had breasts.

TERRACE: I don't think he needed that information Rhoda. I'm sure he assumed I had breasts. Sometimes you're like a man.

RHODA: Because I love your breasts?

TERRACE: No, because you advertise them. Because you sell them.

RHODA: I am completely subjective about your breasts. I have wanted them since I was fifteen and I saw them in the dance locker room.

TERRACE: They weren't just sitting there in the locker room. They were attached to me. Why don't you ever see me Rhoda?

RHODA: I have wanted your breasts Terrace. I used to believe that if I stayed your friend, you would give them to me.

TERRACE: You have the perfect body Rhoda. You have the ultimate flat stomach and your legs go on and on. They disappear under your dress and they create suspense.

RHODA: My breasts are flat. There is nothing to my chest, there is nothing to get at.

TERRACE: Has Mr. Good and Thin developed an emotional vocabulary? I mean is he pre-recovery arrogant shut down seductive 'cause you can't have him macho or has he done ever a little tiny bit of work on himself?

RHODA: Who could tell. A lot of these guys learn the language. They're completely therapized, but they're totally insane. Look at my x-husband. When I asked him why he was sleeping with my sister, why he needed to do that to me, he said he was learning how to take care of himself. His group therapy thought it was a huge breakthrough that he was finally addressing his needs, that he'd stopped people pleasing.

TERRACE: I need to believe there's a reason to go through all this. I don't get men. They're on some course. They don't veer off. They mow the lawn, they bring in wood, they do activities. They get excited peeing in the woods. They tell jokes. They stare off. I know you Rhoda. You bleed. You pick at salads. You can't find things in the bottom of your bag. You lose your keys. You need to talk a lot. You cry at art. You get radical goose bumps when I tickle your arm. Who is this guy, Rhoda? Does he really want to take the big journey? Isn't this first date, whether we say it or not, about deciding, about deciding whether we want to take the big journey with each other? Does any guy really want to take the big journey?

RHODA: You are so intense Terrace and you just asked four questions.

TERRACE: I do not have a flat stomach. In the end that's all that really matters. That's all he'll be thinking about. Is a flat stomach. I'll be brilliant and funny and caring and deep and he'll be thinking about my not flat stomach.

RHODA: No Terrace, that's what you'll be thinking about. You'll be thinking about your not flat stomach and I'll be thinking about my non-existent breasts. We will be thinking about these things because we think everyone is thinking about these things. We will have our focus there and we will not even hear the conversation and because of this we will seem distracted and withholding and this will change everything.

TERRACE: Have you ever considered me, Rhoda? I'm a vegetarian, I'm intense and I do pretty amazing arm.

RHODA: You are definitely the closest thing I've ever found to what I want. Particularly the way you do my arm . . . (*Terrace continues to tickle Rhoda's arm as Rhoda moans and lights fade.*)

KINDERTRANSPORT

Diane Samuels

3 Women

Helga (30–40) a survivor of the Holocaust; Faith; and Eva (16) her daughter.

Scene: A spare room in Evelyn's house in a London suburb, recent times.

Eva's parents were German Jews who sent her to safety in London in the late 1930s. When the war years passed by with no word from her family, Eva assumed they had perished in the camps. Now a British citizen, Eva changed her name to Evelyn and has been adopted by the family that took her in. Following the war, Evelyn's mother, Helga, arrives in London in search of the daughter she never thought to see again. Following an awkward reunion, Helga tells Evelyn that they will now travel to America and make a new life with those of their family who have survived. On the day their boat is scheduled to depart, Evelyn refuses to go. Here, mother and daughter share a moment of grief, accusation, and pain.

O   O   O

(Faith picks up a box and exits. Evelyn carefully sorts through the boxes and objects, placing chosen items neatly together. Sounds of quayside. A boat is about to leave. It is busy, lots of people, noise and activity. Helga is waiting. Eva, very agitated, approaches.)

HELGA: Where have you been?

EVA: I said. In the lavatory.

HELGA: For half an hour in the lavatory?

EVA: I was being sick.

HELGA: Sick?

EVA: I'm all right now.

HELGA: Are you sure?

EVA: Yes.

HELGA: You should change your mind and come with me.

EVA: I haven't got a case.

HELGA: You could have your things sent on.

EVA: You said it was all right to come later.

HELGA: I said I would prefer you to come now. There is enough money from Onkel Klaus for a ticket.

EVA: I can't just leave.

HELGA: Why do you not want to be with your mother Eva?

EVA: Evelyn. My name is Evelyn.

HELGA: Why are you so cold to me?

EVA: I don't mean to be cold.

HELGA: We have been together a week and you are still years away.

EVA: I can't help it. *(Ship's horn sounds.)*

HELGA: Boats do not wait for people.

EVA: I hope you have a safe trip.

HELGA: When is "later" when you are coming?

EVA: In a month or two.

HELGA: Just get on the boat with me. Do it now.

EVA: I'm not ready yet. Not at all.

HELGA: You're making a mistake.

EVA: It's what you're making me…

HELGA: What am I making you do! I am your mother. I love you. We must be together.

EVA: We've not been together for too long.

HELGA: That is why it is even more important now.

EVA: I can't leave home yet.

HELGA: Home is inside you. Inside me and you. It is not a place.

EVA: I don't understand what you mean.

HELGA: You are wasting a chance hardly anyone else has been given.

EVA: I will come.

HELGA: Will you?

EVA: If you want me to.

HELGA: If I want you to?

EVA: Just not yet.

HELGA: Do you want to come to make a new life with me?

EVA: You keep asking me that.

HELGA: Do you?

EVA: It's hard for me.

HELGA: I lost your father. He was sick and they put him in line for the showers. I saw it. You know what I say to you. I lost him. But I did not lose myself. Nearly, a million times over, right on the edge of life, but I held on with my bones rattling inside me. Why have you lost yourself, Eva? *(Ship's horn sounds out.)* I am going to start again. I want my daughter Eva with me. If you find her, Evelyn, by any chance, send her over to find me. *(Helga embraces Eva who stands stock still. Helga picks up her case and starts to walk away. Eva stands shaking silently.)*

EVELYN: *(Quietly.)* There are four types of daughters: wise, bad, stupid and the ones who do not know what to ask.

HELGA: *(Turning round.)* Which are you?

EVELYN: I wish you had died.

HELGA: I wish you had lived.

EVELYN: I did my best.

HELGA: Hitler started the job and you finished it.

EVELYN: Why does it have to be my fault?

HELGA: You cut off my fingers and pulled out my hair one strand at a time.

EVELYN: You were the Ratman. You had his face.

HELGA: You hung me out of the window by my ears and broke my soul into shreds.

EVELYN: You threw me into the sea with all your baggage on my shoulders.

HELGA: You can never excuse yourself.

EVELYN: How could I swim ashore with so much heaviness on me? I was drowning in leagues and leagues of salty water.

HELGA: I have bled oceans out of my eyes.

EVELYN: I had to let go to float.

HELGA: Snake! Slithering out of yourself like it was an unwanted skin. Skinless snake! Worm!

EVELYN: What right have you to accuse me? What right did you have to claim me back and hate me when I couldn't come?

HELGA: My suffering is monumental. Yours is personal. Mine is a mountain. Yours is a tiny mound.

EVELYN: What about what you did to me! *(She starts to lose control.)* You should have hung onto me and never let me go. Why did you send me away when you were in danger? No one made you! You chose to do it. Didn't it ever occur to you that I might have wanted to die with you? Because I did. I never wanted to live without you and you made me! What is more cruel than that? Except for coming back from the dead and punishing me for surviving on my own. *(Evelyn sobs. Faith enters.)*

FAITH: *(To Evelyn.)* Didn't it ever occur to you that I might have wanted to cry with you? *(Faith kneels close by Evelyn and holds onto her back. Evelyn does not turn to face Faith. Helga exits in one direction. Evelyn exits in another.)*

FAITH: Did you used to weep behind closed doors or did you never do it?

EVELYN: Crying doesn't change what happened.

FAITH: What can I do for you? Please tell me what I can do to help?

EVELYN: Stay my little girl forever.

FAITH: I can't.

EVELYN: Then there's nothing you can do. *(Evelyn starts to get up.)*

FAITH: I'm going to find out everything I can. Get in touch with my relatives. I want to meet them.

EVELYN: You'll find them very different.

FAITH: I'm sure they'd love to see you too.

EVELYN: I have nothing in common with them and neither do you.

FAITH: I want that put right.

EVELYN: I don't want you to bring trouble onto yourself.

A PERFECT GANESH

Terrence McNally

2 Women

Katherine and Margaret (50s) two friends traveling together to India.

Scene: An airplane bound for India

Katherine and Margaret are both traveling to India, in search of some kind of spiritual release; Katherine from the guilt she feels over her son's death and Margaret from the fear caused by a lump she has discovered in her breast. The two go back a long way, as can be seen in this scene where Katherine does her best to combat Margaret's fear of flying.

○　　　○　　　○

KATHERINE: Does he remind you of Walter?

MARGARET: The steward? Not in the least.

KATHERINE: I didn't know you were afraid of flying.

MARGARET: I've flown over this part of the Atlantic this time of the year at least fifteen times and it was never like this.

KATHERINE: Actually, I like a little turbulence.

MARGARET: You're the type who would.

KATHERINE: It lets me know we're really up there. If it gets too quiet and still, I worry the engines have stopped and we're just going to plummet to the earth.

MARGARET: Can we talk about something else?

KATHERINE: Do you want to hold my hand?

MARGARET: Of course not.

KATHERINE: Do you want some gum?

MARGARET: Is it the kind that sticks to your crowns?

KATHERINE: I don't know.

MARGARET: If it's the kind that sticks I don't want it.

KATHERINE: You're out of luck. It must have been in the bag I left in the terminal.

MARGARET: What's that?

KATHERINE: A whistle. George made me take it. In case we get in any sort of trouble in India, I'm supposed to blow it so help will come. "Who?" I asked him. "Sabu on an elephant?"

MARGARET: Will you keep your voice down? *(The plane heaves, extra-mightily this time.)*

KATHERINE: This is ridiculous. Give me your hand.

MARGARET: We're all going to die.

KATHERINE: Just shut up and say a "Hail, Mary."

MARGARET: Methodists don't say "Hail, Mary."

KATHERINE: We're going to be all right.

MARGARET: Ow! That's too tight! *(The turbulence subsides.)*

KATHERINE: See?

MARGARET: I can bear anything as long as I know it's going to end.

KATHERINE: Remember the last year we went to St. Kitt's?

MARGARET: The men got sick from eating crayfish.

KATHERINE: They were *langouste*.

MARGARET: They looked like crayfish.

KATHERINE: That's not the reason I never wanted to go back there.

MARGARET: Alan nearly died. Besides, it was a time for a new island.

KATHERINE: It was the incident with the little plane.

MARGARET: What incident? I don't remember.

KATHERINE: Yes, you do. We were swimming in front of the hotel. A small, single-engine plane had taken off from the airport. The engine kept stalling. No one moved. It was terrifying. That little plane just floating there. No sound. No sound at all. Like a kite without a string. I don't think I've ever felt so helpless.

MARGARET: I remember.

KATHERINE: Finally, I guess the pilot made the necessary adjustments, the engine caught and stayed caught and the little plane flew away, as if nothing had happened, and we finished swimming and played tennis and after lunch you bought the Lalique vase I could still kick myself for letting you have.

MARGARET: You've envied me that piece of Lalique all these years? It's yours.

KATHERINE: I don't want it.

MARGARET: Really, I insist, Kitty. I think I only bought it because I knew you wanted it. That, and I was mad at Alan for some crack about how I looked in my new bathing suit. The plane's stopped jiggling. Smooth as glass now.

KATHERINE: I've thought about that little plane a lot. Maybe we were helpless. May be we weren't responsible. Maybe it wasn't our fault. But what kept that plane up there? God? A God? Some Benevolence? Prayer? Our prayers? I think everyone on that beach was praying that morning in their particular way. So maybe we aren't so helpless. Maybe we are responsible. Maybe it is our fault what happens. Maybe, maybe, maybe.

MARGARET: Do you want to give me my hand back?

KATHERINE: I'm sorry. Thank you. Did I do that? I *was* holding tight! I'm sorry. *(She kisses Margaret's hand.)* What happened to your liver spots? You used to have great big liver spots.

MARGARET: Will you keep your voice down? I keep begging you to come with me. The man's a genius. And it's paradise there.

KATHERINE: And it costs three thousand dollars a week. I'd rather go to India for my soul than some spa in Orange County for the backs of my hands.

MARGARET: Happily, you can afford both.

KATHERINE: I keep thinking about Walter.

MARGARET: Why would you do that to yourself?

KATHERINE: I can't help it.

MARGARET: Well, stop. Stop right now. Think about something else. Think about the Taj Mahal. Think about India.

KATHERINE: They say it's like a dream, the Taj Mahal.

MARGARET: I hope it's not like the Eiffel Tower. All your life you look at pictures of the Eiffel Tower and then when you actually see it, it looks just like the pictures of it. There's no resonance when you look at the Eiffel Tower. I'm expecting some resonance from the Taj Mahal. I'll be terribly disappointed if there isn't any. You're humming again, Kitty.

KATHERINE: I'm sorry.

MARGARET: You asked me to tell you.

KATHERINE: All of a sudden, I can't remember when it was built!

MARGARET: It was begun in 1632 and completed in 1654.

KATHERINE: All that reading up on it and for what?

MARGARET: Do you remember who it was built for?

KATHERINE: Of course I do. Someone's wife.

MARGARET: Everyone knows that, Kitty. What was her name?

KATHERINE: I knew you were going to ask me that. Marilyn? Betty? Betty Mahal? I know who built it. Shah Jahan.

MARGARET: The favorite wife was Mumtaz Mahal.

KATHERINE: Mumtaz, of course! It was on the tip of my tongue.

MARGARET: It took twenty-two years and twenty thousand workers to build.

KATHERINE: Is this going to be some sort of pop quiz?

MARGARET: I was trying to get your mind off Walter.

KATHERINE: Nothing will ever get my mind off Walter.

MARGARET: This is a wonderful start to a trip!

KATHERINE: I'm sorry. *(She hums a little.)*

MARGARET: Kitty, sshh!, you're doing it. It's nobody's fault. *(Katherine begins to read from a travel brochure she has taken out of her purse.)*

KATHERINE: Now listen to this. *(She reads.)* "Don't drink the water, which means absolutely no ice in your drinks or eating of washed fruits and vegetables." Sounds charming. "Above all be patient. Allow, accept, be."

MARGARET: That's what I've been telling you.

SUNDAY ON THE ROCKS

Theresa Rebeck

3 Women
Elly, Jen, and Gayle (all around 30) roommates and friends.

Scene: Here and Now

Elly, Jen, and Gayle have spent Sunday morning drinking scotch and trading secrets. Here, the three tipsy women keep the party going with a Ouija board.

(The lights are lowered and the blinds are drawn. A half-filled plate of oatmeal cookies sits on the floor in front of the couch next to a disgustingly full tray of cigarettes. The easy chair has been dragged over to the couch, and Jen and Gayle sit holding a Ouija board on their knees. Elly lounges full length on the couch and watches them. The cursor moves rapidly across the surface of the board.)

JEN: You're pushing it.

GAYLE: I'm not, I swear!

JEN: N—E—Y—Barney. We're talking to Barney, is that right?

GAYLE: *(Watching board.)* Yes.

JEN: I have never had a Ouija board work this good.

GAYLE: What do you want to ask him? Hi, Barney.

JEN: *(Reading.)* H—I. Hi. This is great. Are you sure you're not pushing?

GAYLE: Jen—

ELLY: Barney? We're talking to a male spirit? Wouldn't you know. Tell Barney we don't want to talk to men today.

JEN: Elly, no—shit, she doesn't mean it, Barney. Are you still here? *(She watches.)* Yes. Thank God. *(Elly giggles.)* Stop it, Elly. This is very serious and if he thinks you're a nonbeliever he'll go away. You can't just fool around with this.

ELLY: PLEASE.

JEN: Elly!

ELLY: Okay, okay. I have a question. Ask him—if Gayle's new boyfriend is going to call back.

GAYLE: Elly—

JEN: Yes. It says yes.

GAYLE: You're pushing this—

JEN: I would never push a Ouija—

ELLY: I knew it! I knew it was a guy.

GAYLE: It was just a date.

JEN: Come on, come on, we have to ask him another question. Think of a question.

GAYLE: I want to know—let me think, I want to know—

ELLY: Is there sex in afterlife? *(The cursor moves wildly from one end of the board to the other.)*

JEN: Great. Oh, great. That's what it does when it knows there's an unbeliever present. Barney, no, we believe in you.

ELLY: No, we don't, Barney.

GAYLE: It's saying something. Look, it's spelling something.

JEN: God, we didn't even ask a question. This is amazing— *(Pause. They all watch.)*

GAYLE: Go.

JEN: Go. Go where?

ELLY: Go fish.

JEN: Elly—

GAYLE: No. come on, pay attention, it's saying go outside and do something—

JEN: It's not going to say anything as long as Elly just keeps making fun of it.

GAYLE: Yes, Barney's telling us to get the hell out of here and actually do something; it's a beautiful day out—

JEN: Wait a minute. Wait a minute. You are pushing this, aren't you?

GAYLE: Of course I'm pushing it! For heaven's sake, let's get out of here! We've been lying around all day—

JEN: That's great. That's just great. You guys are both jerks. *(She starts to throw the Ouija board back into the box.)*

ELLY: No, come on, come on, I want to ask it a question.

JEN: Just forget it, Elly. You made your stupid point.

GAYLE: Look, I'm sorry. I just thought—

JEN: You shouldn't fuck around with this, I'm telling you—

ELLY: I'm not fucking around. I have a question. I want to know—I want to know if I can use this thing to talk to my mother.

JEN: Oh, ha ha, that's real funny.

ELLY: I'm not kidding!

JEN: You can only talk to dead people with a Ouija board, moron.

ELLY: No kidding, moron. *(Pause. Gayle takes her hand off the cursor and looks at Jen. They all look at each other.)*

GAYLE: Oh, Jesus, Jen. You're kidding, right?

JEN: Your mother's dead? When did she die?

ELLY: What? Four years ago. Are you kidding? She died four years ago.

JEN: Your mother's dead? You didn't tell me your mother was dead.

ELLY: I've been living with you for a year. How could you not know?

JEN: Why didn't you tell me? *(Pause.)*

ELLY: That is so depressing.

JEN: Well, we don't exactly see each other a lot. Just weekends and shit.

ELLY: Yeah. It just makes you wonder. I mean, who knows what kind of shit we don't know about each other?

GAYLE: Yeah. In between childhood and adulthood.

JEN: God, I know. I mean, like, think about it. How did we meet?

ELLY: God help us all. Jessica picked us.

JEN: That's my point. The three of us, we could be anybody, you know. I saw this movie, where this girl got a roommate through the personals, who tried to *kill* her—

GAYLE: Jen!

JEN: What?

GAYLE: Come back.

JEN: Oh. Sorry. *(Pause.)* So—how'd your mom die?

ELLY: Oh—she was killed in a car accident. Some moron ran a red light at fifty miles an hour and smashed into her. He was driving this Oldsmobile station wagon, and she was in a Chevette. She didn't stand a chance.

JEN: Do you miss her?

ELLY: Oh, yeah.

JEN: That's nice. I mean, it's not nice that she's dead; it's nice that you miss her. If my mother died I think I'd have a party.

GAYLE: Jen!

JEN: What? My mother's a bitch!

GAYLE: Well, my mother's a bitch too, but I wouldn't throw a party.

ELLY: My mother was cool

GAYLE: Yeah?

ELLY: Yeah. She was totally content, you know? I always thought that was amazing. I mean, she did exactly what she wanted to do with her life. She wanted to get married and have babies and raise them, and so that's what she did.

JEN: Raising babies made her content? It drove my mother to drink.

ELLY: No—I mean, yes, but that's not the point. The point is she *wanted* to raise babies. We drove her crazy, but she wanted to be driven crazy by a bunch of kids.

JEN: That doesn't make any sense.

ELLY: The point is she did what she wanted to do.

WOMEN IN FLAMES

Mary Garripoli

2 Women
Annette (17), a young woman questing for freedom, and Doris (36), her mother

Scene: An American living room, July 4, 1969

Annette has stolen several of her mother's bras for the purpose of burning them at a Women's Lib rally. When Doris confronts her daughter regarding the theft of lingerie, accusation leads to revelation.

(*It is the middle of the night. The room is black except for a touch of moonlight coming through a window up center. Annette Cuneo enters stage right through the front door. She is dressed in blue jeans. Unbeknownst to Annette, her mother, Doris Cuneo, is sitting on the other side of the room in the dark. Doris is an attractive 36 year old housewife. Annette opens the front door. Before she can switch on the lights the beam of a high voltage flashlight hits her, focusing its light on her chest area.*)

DORIS: (*From across the room.*) Stay right where you are, don't move a muscle.

ANNETTE: (*At the door.*) Mom?! It's me!

DORIS: I know who it is. Jump!

ANNETTE: Jump?

DORIS: Three inches off the ground, let's go!

ANNETTE: Mother, give me a break! Did you take too many diet pills again? I'm turning on the lights. (*She flips on the light switch to the left of the open door revealing her mother sitting on an armchair down stage right.*)

DORIS: Aha! I knew it! (*Annette closes the door and takes a hard look at her mother.*)

Annette: Mother…

Doris: When you moved just now, I saw it with my own eyes. You're not wearing a bra, are you?!

Annette: Mother?!

Doris: I knew it! I knew it all along! (*Doris puts down the flashlight on the coffee table between them.*) Okay, let's have it! Spit it out! If you're not wearing them, then what have you done with my brassieres?

Annette: Mom, it's the middle of the night. Can we talk about your brassieres in the morning?

Doris: They're my brassieres, I'll talk about them when I want to! …Well… I'm waiting.

Annette: (*Quietly.*) I burned them.

Doris: You what?

Annette: I burned them! …At the Feminist rally outside the mayor's office last Saturday. I burned six of your bras and tied together three of your longline girdles to make a banner!

Doris: You burned my underwear?! In public?! …Did anyone know it was MY underwear?

Annette: Nobody knew! I didn't write your name on 'em!

Doris: Why?! Why did you do it?

Annette: To liberate women from the oppression of men. We have to burn our bras to free ourselves! Is there a better way to celebrate the Fourth of July?

Doris: Is that a real question?

Annette: Go ahead, make a joke! It's easier than listening to me.

Doris: Don't start with me, I always listen to you!

Annette: Bullshit!

Doris: Don't you dare use that language with me!

Annette: Bullshit! I said "Bullshit" because it is bullshit! I'm not a baby anymore! I can talk any way I want to!

Doris: Not in my house.

Annette: Not in your world! Your whole life is this house.

Doris: You think I'm nothing! That I'm not part of life, that I don't count! Well, this time, you went too far.

Annette: Sometimes you have to go far to get what you want!

DORIS: (*Sighing*) Look, I don't wanna fight with you. There's really only one thing I need to know—and I need to know so I can get some sleep, which believe me I also need — why my bras? Why burn my underwear to free yourself?

ANNETTE: Because I only own one bra and I need it for dance class. (*Doris looks at her daughter in amazement as all of this sinks in.*)

DORIS: That is the singularly most selfish thing I have ever heard in my live — except maybe for Liz Taylor breaking up Debbie and Eddie.

ANNETTE: Oh, please…

DORIS: Don't "Oh, please" me! You better come up with something better than "Oh, please!"

ANNETTE: Can we finish talking about this tomorrow? I have to get to bed. They bombed the chem lab last week. I have three experiments to make up tomorrow. (*Annette turns to go up to her room.*)

DORIS: Come back here! You can't go to bed yet. Not with my underwear on your conscience. You owe me an apology.

ANNETTE: For what?

DORIS: For what? For stealing. You took something that was mine. I want remorse!

ANNETTE: Look, I'm sorry, okay! If I knew you were gonna get so bent about this…

DORIS: This is your apology?! This is how you feel when you break a commandment?

ANNETTE: I didn't think of it as stealing.

DORIS: Whatta you call it? Borrowing? It's not borrowing because you can't give them back —except maybe in an urn!

ANNETTE: You really should be thanking me. You needed me to do it.

DORIS: Don't you tell me what I need!

ANNETTE: You're asleep. Somebody had to wake you up.

DORIS: So you're gonna play God and tell me how to think?

ANNETTE: You don't get what I'm about at all. You think this whole thing is about my stealing your underwear… (*Doris starts to in-*

terject but Annette cuts her off) Which I did! Okay, alright!

DORIS: You are five minutes from being grounded!

ANNETTE: Fine, ground me! See if I care! Ground me for life!

DORIS: That's it! Pack up your love beads, you're outta here!

ANNETTE: Fine! But I don't take it back! You're just pissed because you don't get it!

DORIS: You think I'm stupid. You think I don't know about Women's Liberation? I'm a wife and a mother. If that isn't the definition of "slavery" I don't know what is!

ANNETTE: Then join in with me, don't yell at me.

DORIS: What would I be joining?

ANNETTE: What?

DORIS: What? What would I be joining?

ANNETTE: You don't mean it.

DORIS: Annette, I can't fight you anymore. My laugh lines are getting as deep as ravines. Now, what would I be joining?

ANNETTE: Mother, you're a woman — this is Feminism!

DORIS: Okay, so tell me about it. Tell me about Women's Liberation.

ANNETTE: First of all, call it what it is. Feminism. That's what we call it. Men call it Women's Liberation because… well…

DORIS: It's catchier?

ANNETTE: Very funny!

DORIS: Well, it is. It definitely has more of a ring to it.

ANNETTE: You think you're so funny, but you play right into that "Helpless Little Woman" shit!

DORIS: This is what you believe?

ANNETTE: This is what I know. (*Doris goes to pour herself a glass of Sambuca. Annette follows her.*)

ANNETTE: Are you listening to me?

DORIS: Yes.

ANNETTE: I don't feel like you're listening.

DORIS: I'm listening! I am listening! I listen to you more than anybody. I listen to you more than you listen to me —more than your father listens to either of us! Whatta you want, Annette? I can't listen any harder. What do you want? (*The are silent and we hear the "pop" of distant fireworks.*)

ANNETTE: I want to be everything I can be.

DORIS: That's all I ever wanted for you.

ANNETTE: Well… that's what I'm about.

DORIS: It's a good thing to be about. Maybe we're both feminists. Although I still can't see how my frying my underwear in the street is gonna make your father pick his up off the floor.

ANNETTE: See, Mom, that's what I mean about you. You reduce everything down to something stupid.

DORIS: Well, I'm sorry Miss College Student — or should I say, "Ms."? It's the little every day things that life's about, everything can't always be big, important issues.

ANNETTE: There's a lot more going on in the world than your laundry. You get more pissed off about dumb little stuff than you even do about the war. You really oughtta look at that.

DORIS: Don't tell me I don't get pissed about the war! Daddy and I fight about Jane Fonda at least twice a week!

ANNETTE: Daddy's a war monger!

DORIS: No, he isn't. He's a Veteran. When you were born, he bragged for months about how you have the same birthday as Mamie Eisenhower. He's a good guy—if he picked up his fruit of the looms, he'd be almost perfect.

ANNETTE: If it's that important to you, why don't you just ask him?

DORIS: Believe me, the subject has come up several times in the last eighteen years.

ANNETTE: I can't believe that Daddy would just refuse to pick up his underwear.

DORIS: It's not that he refuses, it's more like he can't get it. The same way he can't remember to put the toilet seat down so I don't sit in the water when I go to the bathroom at night. Men are a mystery.

ANNETTE: Men are the same as us.

DORIS: That's Women's Lib talking.

ANNETTE: Mom, you're a fossil. This is 1969, things are different now.

DORIS: They are?

ANNETTE: Of course they are. I'm going to bed.

DORIS: I think I'll sit up a bit for Dad. He went to the fireworks at the V. F. W.

ANNETTE: You always sit up and wait for him. Just once, I wish you'd go out — make him wait up for you. You can walk out the door. You're a free woman.

DORIS: I've heard. But I can also see the fireworks from our window, and that's enough for me, thank you. Good night, Annette. (*Annette starts up to bed and stops again.*)

ANNETTE: I'm sorry about your bras, Mom, I'll get you some new ones.

DORIS: Apology accepted and you don't have to. Goodnight, honey.

ANNETTE: No, I want to. I feel like I hurt you and I'm gonna replace them, okay?

DORIS: Well, okay. But you still don't have to, because your father's gonna buy me all new clothes for our trip.

ANNETTE: What trip?

DORIS: We're going on vacation, him and me.

ANNETTE: You didn't tell me about it.

DORIS: I just decided. Actually, we're going because you burned my bras. (*Annette looks questioningly as Doris continues.*) See, when I went to get dressed this morning, I had to put on my blouse without a bra—we know why, let's not go into it again—and Daddy could tell.

ANNETTE: That you didn't have a bra on? So what?

DORIS: Netta, I don't flounce around without underwear like you do. No woman my age does. We weren't raised like that. I used to wear a girdle to bed before a big date! When your father didn't see a brassiere on me, he knew something was up.

ANNETTE: So…?

DORIS: So you know how he gets. All crazy in his head when he thinks there's something outta his royal domain. So I told him, "I lost all my bras, don't bug me!" So then we had a fight.

ANNETTE: About your bras?

DORIS: About my having an affair. (*Annette is obviously shaken and has to sit down. We hear a loud "boom" offstage.*) You look pale, Annette, go to bed.

ANNETTE: You're kidding, right?

DORIS: No, you look pale.

ANNETTE: What are you doing? You're thirty-six years old!

DORIS: Meaning what? No one would find me attractive?

ANNETTE: You know what I mean!

DORIS: No, I do not know what you mean. I'm not really what? Young anymore? I'm not pretty or sexy... or ALIVE anymore?! No, Annette, I do not know what you mean! Or maybe more to the point, I don't care. (*Doris goes to the window and looks out at the fireworks.*)

DORIS: The fireworks are almost over. Look! Come see them. I love the ones that streak across the moon. Their tales all full of color—like a comet or something. It takes guts to make a splash like that.

ANNETTE: Are you having an affair, Mommy?

DORIS: That's what your father wanted to know.

ANNETTE: Are you?

DORIS: Well, that's nobody's business but mine. I'm a free woman, remember? But since you asked, I'll tell you what I told him. No, I am not having an affair. Of course I still couldn't explain how I'd lost my underwear...

ANNETTE: I'll tell him what happened!

DORIS: You could do that. I wouldn't argue with you. (*Annette stares at Doris in shock and disbelief.*)

ANNETTE: You want him to think you're having an affair...

DORIS: I want a vacation. And... I wouldn't mind if he stayed home a few nights a week... and if once in a while he picked up his underwear. Even if he just did it out of fear. Sometimes you have to go far to get what you want. (*She holds out her hand.*) Come watch the fireworks with me, Annette. (*Blackout.*)

WONDERFUL TENNESSEE

Brian Friel

2 Women
Berna (30–40) a woman recovering from a breakdown, and Angela
(30–40) her sister.

Scene: Ireland

Berna and Anglea are on holiday with their husbands and friends, and
the group has been stranded by the edge of the sea. Anglea takes advantage of their plight to spend a quiet moment with Berna.

○   ○   ○

ANGELA: What's the water like?

BERNA: Warm. Warmish.

ANGELA: Wouldn't mind a swim. Brighten us all up. *(She hugs
Berna quickly.)* And how's the baby sister? *(Berna shrugs.)*
You're looking much stronger.

BERNA: Am I?

ANGELA: Terry says you'll be back in the practice in a month.

BERNA: That's not true. Who's looking after the children tonight?

ANGELA: The McGuires next door.

BERNA: The whole brood?

ANGELA: I know. Hearts of gold.

BERNA: I have a birthday present for young Frankie. I'll drop it in at
the weekend.

ANGELA: You have that godson of yours spoiled.

BERNA: No, I'll get Terry to leave it in. The godson has got very…
tentative with me recently.

ANGELA: You couldn't make that—

BERNA: I make him uneasy. You know how intuitive children are. I
think maybe I frighten him.

ANGELA: Frankie's dying about you, Berna.

BERNA: Frighten is too strong. When I reach out to touch him he shrinks away from me. I... disquiet him. Anyhow. Do you really think I look stronger?

ANGELA: I know you are.

BERNA: Terry thinks the reason for my trouble is that we couldn't have a child. That's what he tells the doctors. And that never worried me all that much. But it's an obsession with him. He's even more neurotic than Trish about not having children. A Martin neurosis, I tell him.

ANGELA: Shhh.

BERNA: And he would have been so good with children. Married the wrong sister, didn't he?

ANGELA: Berna—

BERNA: Oh, yes; oh, yes. When you married Frank a little portion of him atrophied. Then he turned to me. I'm the surrogate.

ANGELA: You've got to—

BERNA: Are you happy, Angela? *(Angela hums "Happy days are here again.")* There are times when I feel I'm... about to be happy. That's not bad, is it? Are you laughing at me?

ANGELA: Of course I'm not laughing at you.

BERNA: Maybe that's how most people manage to carry on— "about to be happy"; the real thing *almost* within grasp, just a step away. Maybe that's the norm. But then there are periods— occasions—when just being alive is... unbearable.

The Best
Men's Scenes
# of 1994

THE APPRENTICE

Jack Gilhooley

2 Men
Jamie (20s) an idealistic young playwright, and VanDerveer (30–40) a jaded artistic director.

Scene: Hackensack

Jamie is desperate to have his first play produced—by anyone. Here, he meets with the sleazy artistic director of a small theatre in New Jersey.

○   ○   ○

(Jamie is seated at a desk across from Rance VanDerveer. There are manuscripts lying about. A desk placard reads "Artistic Director.")

JAMIE: …and so, I was really attracted to your philosophy. Which is why I submitted the play, Mr. VanDerveer.

VANDERVEER: Call me Rance. Better yet, call me Vandy. All my friends do.

JAMIE: *(Shaking hands.)* And call me Jamie.

VANDERVEER: When did you submit the play?

JAMIE: Three years ago. I was in New York on spring break. The other kids went to Florida but I had just finished my first play and… well, I put in some overtime at the 7–11 and hitchhiked to New York.

VANDERVEER: Three years ago, huh? Hmmm, we were still on the Lower East Side.

JAMIE: You sure were. You were between a grocery and—

VANDERVEER: A bodega. Actually it was a bordello.

JAMIE: —and a storefront church.

VANDERVEER: A crack house.

JAMIE: I saw a play there. I met your literary manager. She said she'd read my play and get back in a week.

VANDERVEER: Yeah, we pride ourselves on our punctuality. When did she get back?

JAMIE: Never. I passed your theatre last week in my cab. It was pad-locked. Nonpayment of taxes.

VANDERVEER: An oversight. We're nonprofit. Why would we pay taxes on a loss? *(Suddenly alarmed.)* Hey! How did you find us over here?

JAMIE: I had the old program. I looked up the woman in the phone book. Natasha Smolenkovich. She told me you were in Hacken-sack.

VANDERVEER: Hmmmmm. Can't place her. All in black, this chick? Makeup… fingernails… eyeshadow? Eyes themselves?

JAMIE: No, I don't recall that. I'd've remembered a woman with black eyes. Were they contact lenses? How could you see out of black contact len—

VANDERVEER: Nah. Black eyes for real. This chick had a boyfriend that whacked her around all the time. *(Slamming his fist into his palm.)* BAM! BAM! Not unwarranted, I should add. Always mouthing off. Her name was Shirley. She lived with a biker.

JAMIE: Your literary manager lived with a biker?

VANDERVEER: Their clubhouse was up the street. He took a liking to Shirley. One night, he just came in and dragged her off.

JAMIE: Wow! Didn't anyone try to stop him?

VANDERVEER: Nah. She loved it. Anyway, we're artists. Our commit-ment to the human condition begins and ends on stage. Our seamstress asked for her back but the biker threatened to wreck the theatre. We worked it out.

JAMIE: He let her go?

VANDERVEER: No, she stayed. She really got into it down here. When we were leaving for New Jersey, Bruno and his buddies asked if we'd take her with us. We said, "Nothin' doin', fellas. She's un-strung now. This dame would get high sniffing toxic waste. She'd be a carrier of shopping mall blight."

JAMIE: No, this woman wasn't named Shirley. She was—

VANDERVEER: Three years ago, huh? Big tits?

JAMIE: Uh… I didn't notice, actually.

VANDERVEER: Well, then she didn't have big tits. If she did, they'd've been conspicuous, huh? You notice tits on girls, huh?

JAMIE: Well, …y'know, yeah. I mean, that's who they look best on. But it is not how I categorize—

VANDERVEER: Hey, if the shoe fits… Fat legs, speaking of shoes?

JAMIE: She sat behind a desk. I couldn't tell.

VANDERVEER: That should've tipped you off. Why did she sit behind the desk? This is not IBM. We are very flexible, workwise. She could've put her feet up on the desk. She could've sat on the desk. She could've folded her legs… swung 'em… spread 'em apart, even. Hey, did you see that movie where this chick was being interrogated by the cops and there was this absolutely nongratuitous shot where—

JAMIE: Look, I was not attracted to her physical attributes. I was impressed with her vision.

VANDERVEER: We've never had anyone with vision.

JAMIE: She said that The Bloodletters was a company thoroughly dedicated to the total destruction of theatrical representationalism. You were committed to abstract, multidimensional, aesthetically outrageous works that detonate the constricting boundaries of avant-garde radicalism.

VANDERVEER: I'm starting to recall—

JAMIE: She was also against the clutter and chaos of stage minimalism. She said your philosophical models were Nietzsche, Schopenhauer, The Church of Scientology, and the Southwest mystic, David Koresh.

VANDERVEER: Natasha! A real ball-buster, that one! She split. She had her moles removed and found a new lease on life. Changed her name to Bambi Bright. She's writing a prime-time sitcom about two career girls in love with a radiologist.

JAMIE: Did she mention my play before she left?

VANDERVEER: David Koresh. There's a dude who really blew it. All those chicks. He musta been hung like a horse.

JAMIE: *(Rising and heading off.)* I think I made a mistake submitting to The Bloodletters.

VANDERVEER: Whoa! What makes you say that?

JAMIE: Three years ago, I was an unproduced, unpublished playwright. I was fairly flexible.

VanDerveer: And you're still unproduced and unpublished. Are you still fairly flexible?

Jamie: Now, I'd do anything. I'd grovel, even. That's why I should leave.

VanDerveer: Anything? You should be talking to our dramaturg.

Jamie: What's a dramaturg?

VanDerveer: I dunno. The dramaturg doesn't even know. It's a title that looks good on grant applications. What's your play about?

Jamie: Well, ostensibly it's about basketball.

VanDerveer: There's already a play about basketball.

Jamie: There's already a play about everything.

VanDerveer: Not midgets. It's too tough to cast midgets. Basketball. Five characters?

Jamie: Seventeen characters.

VanDerveer: Hold on, sonny. You'd better learn the rudiments of the game before you try your hand at—

Jamie: Five of them tall men.

VanDerveer: Oh, then it's about more than basketball. Are the five guys black?

Jamie: It's irrelevant. They could be white.

VanDerveer: Irrelevant? Is it about a good team or a bad team?

Jamie: A good team.

VanDerveer: Then they're black. They'd only be bad if they were *real* good. Baaaaaaad! But I see what you mean. Maybe black and white is irrelevant. Where'd you learn your playwriting, boy?

Jamie: A little place in South Dakota. Algonquin College.

VanDerveer: Algonquin. That's Indian?

Jamie: An Indian name, yeah. But—

VanDerveer: Are you Indian??? Make the basketball team Indian. If you're Indian, maybe we could get a grant.

Jamie: Do I look Indian?

VanDerveer: No, but they don't need a picture on the grant application. And you were born here in the states, right? A true "Native American"?

Jamie: Sorry, I can't be a part of financial aid under false pretenses.

VANDERVEER: Why not? We make bogus proposals all the time.

JAMIE: And do you get funded?

VANDERVEER: Not yet. We haven't lied big enough. But now we've applied for a grant to do an antinuclear play in Chernobyl.

JAMIE: I doubt if Chernobyl needs an antinuclear play.

VANDERVEER: That's what we figure. So we won't go. We'll use the money to buy a company car. The grant committee won't send an on-site evaluator to Chernobyl. But until then, we can't afford more than four actors.

JAMIE: Afford? You mean you pay?

VANDERVEER: We pay everyone. It's not a lot but it's a closing night lump sum.

JAMIE: Gee, this could be my first income as a playwright.

VANDERVEER: When I said *everyone,* I didn't mean the playwright. They're different so they get compensated differently. After salaries, expenses, and break-even, he gets a small piece of the profits.

JAMIE: Which profits? The ones the IRS is after?

VANDERVEER: The ones *we* declare. Our profits are our business.

JAMIE: Well, I won't suffer from the artist's fatal overindulgences. I'll be too poor to buy a beer. How big is your theatre?

VANDERVEER: You haven't seen our theatre?

JAMIE: No, when I came in today, I waited in the lobby.

VANDERVEER: What lobby?

JAMIE: The room with the two benches. And the platform.

VANDERVEER: You *have* seen the theatre.

JAMIE: You call that a theatre?

VANDERVEER: We call it functional. If you have another outlet, go ahead and—

JAMIE: On the other hand, a space like that stretches one's ingenuity. Four characters, huh?

VANDERVEER: Editing is not hard. You can't get good actors for smaller roles. Eliminate 'em. Put exposition on the radio. Leave speeches on answering machines. Insert phone calls.

JAMIE: Gee, technology could someday make the actor obsolete.

VANDERVEER: The sooner the better. Are you a pro? Is your ingenuity ready for stretching? What would Shakespeare have done with the telephone?

JAMIE: Probably nothing. I don't suppose you'd be able to commission me.

VANDERVEER: After we've all hit it big.

JAMIE: Then I won't need the commission.

VANDERVEER: Well, we need the play pronto!

JAMIE: How pronto?

VANDERVEER: Monday.

JAMIE: Next Monday?

VANDERVEER: Last Monday. We're already in our first rehearsal week.

JAMIE: With my play?

VANDERVEER: With no play. We're waiting for a four-character epic. If you can cut and paste it down from seventeen.

JAMIE: Okay, I've always felt that my play wasn't a play until it was performed. Even if it's not my play being performed.

VANDERVEER: Fine. I'll set you up with our literary manager. A very together babe. Killer legs. *(Winking.)* The rest is up to you.

JAMIE: One thing. I've got someone in mind for the female lead.

VANDERVEER: Sorry. We've got our own company. Maybe for a future production.

JAMIE: Well, I withdraw my play then.

VANDERVEER: Oho, young Chekov is in a snit. Do you have a picture of your little Bernhardt?

JAMIE: You bet. *(He produces an envelope and withdraws Heather's 8x10 glossy. The résumé is on the back but Vandy ignores it.)*

VANDERVEER: She looks right.

JAMIE: Yeah, we think…—uh, I think so.

VANDERVEER: How does she feel about nudity?

JAMIE: There's no nudity in my play.

VANDERVEER: Can you think about something other than *your* play? What about *our* production? This girl is no mere instrument of your egofulfillment. Or any other kind of fulfillment.

JAMIE: Well, if it's artistically viable…

VANDERVEER: Swell, what's her phone number?

JAMIE: It's on the back. Along with her credits.

VanDerveer: Hey, that's a nifty idea, putting info on the back. Is she available this weekend?

Jamie: I'd hoped she'd be with me this weekend.

VanDerveer: Hey Jerry, you've got your work cut out for you. *(Jamie rises to exit. Vandy extends his hand.)* I think we're onto something. You're a rare bird, kid.

Jamie: *(Shaking hands.)* How's that, Vandy?

VanDerveer: A playwright who listens to reason.

ARCADIA
Tom Stoppard

2 Men
  Septimus Hodge (22) a tutor, and Ezra Chater (30–40) a poet.

Scene: A large country house in Derbyshire, 1809

Septimus has been having an affair with Ezra's wife. When the infuri-ated poet demands satisfaction, wily Septimus provides him with just that.

SEPTIMUS: Now, sir, what is this business that cannot wait?

CHATER: I think you know it, sir. You have insulted my wife.

SEPTIMUS: Insulted her? That would deny my nature, my conduct, and the admiration in which I hold Mrs. Chater.

CHATER: I have heard of your admiration, sir! You insulted my wife in the gazebo yesterday evening!

SEPTIMUS: You are mistaken. I made love to your wife in the gazebo. She asked me to meet her there, I have her note some-where, I dare say I could find it for you, and if someone is putting it about that I did not turn up, by God, sir, it is a slan-der.

CHATER: You damned lecher! You would drag down a lady's repu-tation to make a refuge for your cowardice. It will not do! I am calling you out!

SEPTIMUS: Chater! Chater, Chater, Chater! My dear friend!

CHATER: You dare call me that. I demand satisfaction!

SEPTIMUS: Mrs. Chater demanded satisfaction and now you are de-manding satisfaction. I cannot spend my time day and night sat-isfying the demands of the Chater family. As for your wife's reputation, it stands where it ever stood.

CHATER: You blackguard!

SEPTIMUS: I assure you. Mrs. Chater is charming and spirited, with a pleasing voice and a dainty step, she is the epitome of all the qualities society applauds in her sex—and yet her chief renown is for a readiness that keeps her in a state of tropical humidity as would grow orchids in her drawers in January.

CHATER: Damn you, Hodge, I will not listen to this! Will you fight or not?

SEPTIMUS: *(Definitively.)* Not! There are no more than two or three poets of the first rank now living, and I will not shoot one of them dead over a perpendicular poke in a gazebo with a woman whose reputation could not be adequately defended with a platoon of musketry deployed by rota.

CHATER: Ha! You say so! Who are the others? In your opinion?— no—no—!—this goes very ill, Hodge. I will not be flattered out of my course. You say so, do you?

SEPTIMUS: I do. And I would say the same to Milton were he not already dead. Not the part about his wife, of course—

CHATER: But among the living? Mr. Southey?

SEPTIMUS: Southey I would have shot on sight.

CHATER: *(Shaking his head sadly.)* Yes, he has fallen off. I admired "Thalaba" *quite,* but "Madoc," *(He chuckles.)* oh dear me!—but we are straying from the business here—you took advantage of Mrs. Chater, and if that were not bad enough, it appears every stableboy and scullery maid on the strength—

SEPTIMUS: Damn me! Have you not listened to a word I said?

CHATER: I have heard you, sir, and I will not deny I welcome your regard, God knows one is little appreciated if one stands outside the coterie of hacks and placemen who surround Jeffrey and the *Edinburgh*—

SEPTIMUS: My dear Chater, they judge a poet by the seating plan of Lord Holland's table!

CHATER: By heaven, you are right! And I would very much like to know the name of the scoundrel who slandered my verse drama "Maid of Turkey" in the *Piccadilly Recreation,* too!

SEPTIMUS: "The Maid of Turkey"! I have it by my bedside! When I cannot sleep I take up "'The Maid of Turkey" like an old friend!

CHATER: *(Gratified.)* There you are! And the scoundrel wrote he would not give it to his dog for dinner were it covered in bread sauce and stuffed with chestnuts. When Mrs. Chater read that, she wept, sir, and would not give herself to me for a fortnight—which recalls me to my purpose—

SEPTIMUS: The new poem, however, will make your name perpetual—

CHATER: Whether it do or not—

SEPTIMUS: It is not a question, sir. No coterie can oppose the acclamation of the reading public. "The Couch of Eros" will take the town.

CHATER: Is that your estimation?

SEPTIMUS: It is my intent.

CHATER: Is it, is it? Well, well! I do not understand you.

SEPTIMUS: You see I have an early copy—sent to me for review. I say review, but I speak of an extensive appreciation of your gifts and your rightful place in English literature.

CHATER: Well, I must say. That is certainly... You have written it?

SEPTIMUS: *(Crisply.)* Not yet.

CHATER: Ah. And how long does...?

SEPTIMUS: To be done right, it first requires a careful rereading of your book, of both your books, several readings, together with outlying works for an exhibition of deference or disdain as the case merits. I make notes, of course, I order my thoughts, and finally, when all is ready and I am *calm in my mind...*

CHATER: *(Shrewdly.)* Did Mrs. Chater know of this before she—before you—

SEPTIMUS: I think she very likely did.

CHATER: *(Triumphantly.)* There is nothing that woman would not do for me! Now you have an insight to her character. Yes, by God, she is a wife to me, sir!

SEPTIMUS: For that alone, I would not make her a widow.

CHATER: Captain Brice once made the same observation!

SEPTIMUS: Captain Brice did?

CHATER: Mr. Hodge, allow me to inscribe your copy in happy anticipation. Lady Thomasina's pen will serve us.

SEPTIMUS: Your connection with Lord and Lady Croom you owe to your fighting her ladyship's brother?

CHATER: No! It was all nonsense, sir—a canard! But a fortunate mistake, sir. It brought me the patronage of a captain of His Majesty's Navy and the brother of a countess. I do not think Mr. Walter Scott can say as much, and here I am, a respected guest at Sidley Park.

SEPTIMUS: Well, sir, you can say you have received satisfaction.

CANNED GOODS
Silas Jones

2 Men

Angel (60) and Asian-American merchant, and Frank (28) his son.

Scene: King's Market in South Central Los Angeles

Angel has run King's Market for thirty-five years. Today he is turning the business over to Frank, his MBA-toting son who has grandiose ideas of transforming the little neighborhood market into a slick and impersonal convenience store. Angel is having a difficult time letting go and is discovered "preaching" in an evangelical style to an empty store by Frank, who quickly whisks the older man to a shrink's office. When they return to the store, Angel announces that he's changed his mind about selling Frank the business.

o   o   o

(Same day, early afternoon. The market is closed. Angel enters from the back, tosses his sweater onto the counter and immediately begins to rearrange the cans on the shelves. Frank enters presently looking exhausted.)

FRANK: Dad—what are you doing? Everything's—

ANGEL: I know, "systematically arranged." But Angel's crazy, he don't know better. Ain't that what psychiatrist say?

FRANK: He says you're afraid to let go, afraid to face the future. It's a common stress for older people about to retire.

ANGEL: *(Almost breaks down.)* "How long your wife been deceased? When you last had sex?" Personal! I don't know him. "Do you hate Negroes? Do you feel they're out to get you?" Out to get me! "Are you really Asian? You could pass for colored. Some Jews are colored." What I care 'bout Jews! What I care 'bout— "How much significance do you attach to your name?" He crazy! Why you put your father through that? He not even Asian! Why you make me feel like I do something wrong? Like stupid foreigner.

FRANK: Dad, you should have seen yourself! You were preaching, Dad, preaching. Do you always do this? Am I missing something here?

ANGEL: You miss everything! You no come to store till I sell to you. You think I crazy 'cause I talk to self? You not here no time, who I talk to?

FRANK: Preaching, Dad, preaching like a—Dad—sometimes I think—You were acting like one of them. I mean, for the last thirty-five years you've practically lived and breathed—

ANGEL: You know what, I think you crazy. I think UCLA made you crazy. I think your mother—

FRANK: Come on Dad, I'll take you home.

ANGEL: Angel's home, you go home. I'm hungry. I cook the way used to. I go cook.

FRANK: Dad, wait…

ANGEL: Give him good strong Asian name, I told her. She hate America. She hate herself. She name you Frank, you name your son Jonathan, your daughter Heather. Why you let Heather dye hair blond, huh? She only four years old.

FRANK: Five. Dad, her mother is blond, remember?

ANGEL: Someday Heather marry Bob Smith, name son Joe, Joe join Army, get shipped to Asia, war break out, G.I. Joe end up shooting me. Just another old gook on wrong side of conflict. I go cook, I'm hungry.

FRANK: Come on Dad, you'll stink up the place. Let's go home.

ANGEL: Go! Leave Angel alone. I'm very hungry. I cook the way I used to. Place smell good, customers come ask for taste, for recipe. They buy lots of food to cook. Garlic, soy sauce—

FRANK: Dad, this is becoming problematic. I'm not leaving without you.

ANGEL: "I'm not leaving without you." Sound like line out of Casablanca. How come you never learn to speak Korean? Speak Chinese? How come you never come to store with your dad? You 'shamed of Angel, hunh? Everybody ask, "Where your boy? How come we never see him?" I say you visit Grandpa in Korea. I say you sick. I say you got part-time job. I say—I go cook now.

FRANK: Dad, you don't speak Korean or Chinese either, remember? As a matter of fact, I have no idea where you picked up your pidgin English. You don't even have any Asian friends. All right, okay Dad, truce?

ANGEL: Damn "All right, okay!" How come you no like black people? I teach you that? Your momma teach you that? Who teach you that? Who you think you are?

FRANK: You couldn't understand, Dad. You've been hiding out in this American jungle, an Asian exile in somebody else's virtual reality.

ANGEL: Who you think you are, boy! Answer me! Your father is speaking to you!

FRANK: How could you possibly believe that these people love you? To them you're just a lovable old gook.

ANGEL: Silence! *(He is out of control.)* Come—here!

FRANK: All right, Dad, all right. Calm down. I'm sorry, I apolo—.

ANGEL: On your knees! Crawl to your father. Show respect. *(Frank steps to the phone and dials.)* Listen to your father! Your father—

FRANK: This is Frank King, I just left your office. Will you ask Dr. Steinfelt to come to the phone please. *(Angel rushes Frank and snatches the receiver away from him.)* Dad come on, give me the phone. *(Angel yanks out the cord and throws the receiver to the floor.)*

ANGEL: "Dad come on, give me the phone." Foreigner! Why you no love me?

FRANK: Love—? Jesus, Dad, I can't believe we're having this conversation. I thought you were proud of me?

ANGEL: Proud? MBA? My black ass! I wanted to be proud of son, not MBA. All these years I wait for my son. I look for you, you not there. I watch, I pray someday I look up and see my son. At night I come in your room, you sleep, I kiss you on cheek, you wake, look at me like—like I nigger!—slide down under covers. Where go my son? *(Pause.)* You go home now, Angel open up. Thirty-five years I stay open, only day close your mother died. You go home to your family, I stay here. You come back tomorrow take chimes, they yours, family tradition, but that's all. I no sell my life to foreigner.

FRANK: Dad, you're an orphan, remember? You bought the chimes in a pawn shop. *(Beat.)* You want me—You want me to apologize for not being an Asian stereotype. I'm an American stereotype, Dad, born and bred in the U.S. of A. Just like you. No matter how hard you try, Dad, you'll never be like mother. You'll never be Asian. And you'll never be black. *(Angel slaps Frank.)* Welcome to Babylon.

ANGEL: I did not sell you what I feel and think. Get out. My heart not open for business.

FRANK: I didn't want this! I never wanted this! You begged me to take it, remember? Tradition, you said. I thought you needed the money. I've invested over sixty thousand dollars in your little imaginary tradition. Do you understand? The business is mine now, Dad. It's a done deal. It's all legal.

ANGEL: So sue me. Let the door hit you where the good Lord split you. *(Angel opens the door. Chimes ring. Angel turns his back to Frank.)* I don't know you. You don't know me. You don't like me. I don't like you. Nothing personal. Please leave me alone.

(Frank walks past Angel out into the street.)

CUTE BOYS IN THEIR UNDERPANTS FIGHT THE EVIL TROLLS

Robert Coles

2 Men
> Zolnar (30–40) Prince of the trolls, and Todd (20s) a cute boy looking for a job.

Scene: A talent agency which is, in reality, a front for the evil trolls

Todd has responded to Zolnar's ad for a general audition. Little does he suspect that the Prince of the evil trolls plans to take over the world by capturing all the cute boys! Here, unsuspecting Todd "auditions" for the ruthless Zolnar.

O   O   O

ZOLNAR: Are you a performer and/or model, young man?

TODD: Yes, Mr. Zolnar. I have an audition monologue that I could do for you.

ZOLNAR: That won't be necessary just yet. Look off that way for me, please. *(Todd turns and looks where indicated.)* No, *up.* Up and far away. *There.* Right *there.* (Zolnar comes up behind Todd and points.) That spot. That spot way, way off in the distance. Do you see it?

TODD: Yes.

ZOLNAR: You do? Where? That's a wall. Just kidding. *Look!* Look at that spot way, way off in the distance. *(Todd looks avidly. Zolnar steps back and regards Todd shrewdly.)* Very good. Very good. Now… the spot moves! It's… *there* now! *(Zolnar points at the new location for the "spot." Todd looks at the new spot. Zolnar steps back and regards Todd shrewdly.)* Good. Good. Now… the spot is dipping, dipping, *lowering* on the horizon. *(Todd drops his gaze to follow the "spot.")* Tousle your hair.

(Todd tousles.) That's it. Let it drop across your forehead. Don't lose the spot! There it is! *(Zolnar points. Todd's gaze zeroes in on it.)* *Low* on the horizon. Very low. Okay, now. The spot is someone you love. *Love* the spot! *(Todd changes expressions.)* Yes, good. *Love* it. *Cruise* the spot. Say, "Come here, Baby. I want you, Spot. I need you, Spot. Love me, Spot." Now, pout. Go ahead, pout. Give me the lip thing. *(Todd sticks out his lips and pouts.)* Keep the hair tousled. *(Todd tousles.)* Cruise the spot. Say, "Oh, Baby, Baby, I want you, Spot."

TODD: Oh, Baby, Baby, I want—

ZOLNAR: No. Say it with your *Facial expression*.

TODD: Oh. Sorry.

ZOLNAR: Say it with your *look*. Your *look*. Your *look* is *everything*. Now say it: "I love you, Spot. I want you, Spot. Spot, want me. See Spot want. Want, Spot, want." Heh, heh. Just kidding. *Don't* take your eyes off it. That spot is *yours*. Good, good. Now, remove your clothing, please. *(Todd hesitates.)* You *are* interested in catalogue work, aren't you?

TODD: Uh, yes. *(He begins to undress.)*

ZOLNAR: Even for the soaps. It's a must, these days. A good body is a necessity. It's one of your tools. A performer and/or model's tools. An asset. It's part of the product. The total package. The total package of what you offer to the client. When we say "talent," we mean the total package. You mustn't be embarrassed when they ask to see it. They have a right. It's simply that they want to see the total package. You wouldn't expect them to buy a pig in a poke… so to speak. You must be prepared for them to ask. And then present yourself as professionally as possible. *(Todd has stripped to his briefs and socks.)*

TODD: Is this enough, Mr. Zolnar?

ZOLNAR: For now. All right. See the spot! It's down here now. Beneath you. *Now!* Cruise the spot! Cruise with your *full body* now! Use all your tools! The total package! Remember, tousled hair! *(Todd tousles.)* Lips! Lips! *(Todd pouts.)* And body! Hands carefully placed. *(Todd places his hands at different levels on his hips.)* And…shift weight! *(Todd shifts his weight to the other leg, while changing the position of his hands.)* Excellent! Excellent! *(Zolnar, who has placed himself on the floor where the "spot" was supposed to be, suddenly moves.)* Now! The spot is...here! *(Todd changes position to follow the "spot.")* Good! Good! Now...one arm casually over your shoulder. Like this. *(Zolnar demonstrates. Todd does it.)* Now...throw back your head in carefree laughter.

TODD: Ha, ha, ha, ha, ha, ha, ha.

ZOLNAR: You don't need to actually laugh.

TODD: Oh. Sorry.

ZOLNAR: Okay, turn. Your back is to the spot. *(Todd turns.)* Hands on hips. *(Todd does so.)* And...look over your shoulder at the spot! *(Todd does.)* Carefree laughter! *(Todd laughs with no sound.)* Once again! And this time, laugh *as* you turn. *(Todd turns his head away, then looks over his shoulder at the "spot," laughing soundlessly as he turns.)* Excellent! Excellent! Good work! Very well, that's all I need to see.

TODD: Don't you want to hear my monologue?

ZOLNAR: Oh. Oh, certainly.

TODD: It's classical.

ZOLNAR: That's fine. *(Zolnar sits. Todd takes a moment of preparation, then begins.)*

TODD: Oh, that this too too solid flesh would melt, Thaw, and resolve itself into a dew!

ZOLNAR: Good, good. Well, that's fine. We'd like to sign you. *(Todd, still disconcerted that he only got out 15 seconds of his monologue, is startled.)*

TODD: Sign me?

ZOLNAR: Miss Zamphuna has a contract for you. *(She presents it. Todd signs.)*

ZOLNAR: Good. And now... Bwa-ha-ha-ha-ha-ha-ha-ha-ha ! ! ! ! ! I have you in my clutches! Bwa-ha-ha-ha-ha-ha-ha ! ! ! ! ! ! !

TODD: Excuse me?

ZOLNAR: What you don't understand, my pretty, is this: *I am Zolnar, Prince of the Troll People ! ! ! ! ! !*

TODD: Huh?

ZOLNAR: *I am Zolnar, Prince of the Troll People ! ! ! !*

TODD: Yes, you said that.

ZOLNAR: You have become my property! I possess you, as surely as the night owns the day, whatever that means.

THE GATE OF HEAVEN
Lane Nishikawa and Victor Talmadge

2 Men
Kiyoshi "Sam" Yamamoto (30–40) a Japanese-American WW II veteran, and Leon Ehrlich (30–40) his best friend.

Scene: America, 1967

In 1945, Sam was a soldier in the 522nd Artillery of the 442, a division that helped to liberate Dachau. On that day in April, Sam saved the life of Leon Ehrlich, one of the many thousands of prisoners set free by the allies. Years later the two men meet again in the United States and become best of friends, sharing their lives and cultural heritage. SAM, a self-proclaimed "Buddahead," has chosen to celebrate his son's 13th birthday with an unusual Bar Mitzvah. Here, Sam and Leon take a moment during the festivities to discuss tradition and the future.

O   O   O

(Sound fades in with a children's party and the Leon's voice over.)

LEON: A young Talmudic scholar left Minsk and went to America. After many years he returned to the old country. His elderly mother could hardly recognize him. He was dressed in the very latest fashion. "Where is your beard?" his mother asked. The young scholar replied, "Nobody wears a beard in America." The mother then asked, "But at least you keep the Sabbath?" "In America almost everybody works on the Sabbath." She asked hopefully, "And how is the food?" "Ah, mama, it's too much trouble to be kosher in America." The old mother hesitated. Then she whispered, "Tell your old mother, son, are you still circumcised?"

(Sound continues with Sam's laughter, Leon and Steven's voice over.)

LEON: You like that one, huh?

[STEVEN: Today I am a man.] *(Lights fade up on Sam and Leon as they enter.)*

SAM: You want some more cake?

LEON: I've already had two pieces.

SAM: How about some more saké? You can never have enough saké. Ruby's heating it up.

LEON: Ahzisi punim.

SAM: I love that woman. *(They both put their fingers to their lips and kiss like a French chef.)*

SAM: *(With Leon.)* What a gal!

LEON: *(With Sam.)* What a gal! *(They both laugh.)*

SAM: So, how'd you like my son's Bar Mitzvah?

LEON: Schmooks, it was a lovely…ceremony.

SAM: This was a great idea of yours, Leon. Did you see the look on Steven's face when he opened up the box and took out the BB gun?

LEON: I really think the BB gun was a little too much.

SAM: Or when I put the beanie on his head? I know it didn't fit quite right, but I didn't know what size to get.

LEON: Schmookie, size doesn't matter.

SAM: He should have read a passage in Jewish.

LEON: It's Hebrew.

SAM: But the haiku poem. That should count for something, right?

LEON: I didn't understand it.

SAM: Okay, I know it wasn't a real Jewish Bar Mitzvah, but…

LEON: Schmookie, it was a wonderful ceremony.

SAM: …but when you first told me about this way of… I just thought… that Steven might… what I mean is… I don't know… here, we don't have anything like it. In Japan, you're welcomed into the community. In America, because we're Japanese, we're not embraced as men. *(Pause.)* My father and I hardly ever spoke to each other. I have memories of him being tender with me only when I was a baby, like a mother tiger, caring for her cubs, then slapping them away. I had to learn to fight harder, work harder, to be accepted. I don't want Steven to go through what I did. *(Pause.)* I want it to be different with us. I want him to know that I'm there for him. You know what I mean, Leon?

LEON: I understand.

SAM: Hey, wasn't that cute when he turned to you and said, "Thank you for the savings bond, Uncle Leon."

LEON: Let's go outside. I need to talk to you. *(Leon crosses.)*

SAM: I know it wasn't exactly like you wanted it to be.

LEON: Sam. I'm thinking about … going away.

SAM: You're going down South again? This time you're going to join Reverend King, right? Well, this time you're going to get yourself hanged. 'Cause you know they hate white people who help Negroes. And you know they hate Jews.

LEON: No. It's a war.

SAM: Vietnam?

LEON: Israel.

SAM: Well… then you have to go.

LEON: You think so?

SAM: They're your people. You have to help them.

LEON: I know.

SAM: You're going as a doctor, right?

LEON: Yes, but…

SAM: What but? What's the problem?

LEON: I don't know. It feels different this time.

SAM: Arabs.

LEON: I'll be fighting my own family, Sam.

SAM: What do you mean?

LEON: Arabs and Jews are cousins. Both Arabs and Jews call Abraham their father. This is a blood feud within a family. This war is also about land. It's about who has a right to exist on that land. It's about who has a god-given right to a homeland.

SAM: So, what's stopping you?

LEON: I don't want to see anymore people die.

SAM: Leon, you'll be going to see how many you can save. *(Pause.)* Leon, you remember what today stands for? Bar Mitzvah means, "Son of a good deed." You told me, the deed of becoming a man is accepting responsibility to his community.

LEON: How to live together. It was God's gift. Moses was the first to teach us that. (*Pause.*) Sam, I believe we must strive to encompass the all of life, the dark and the light, and embrace everything we can. And if we can't embrace this duality... we are never whole and never able to truly share with others. Otherwise we become what we resist. (*Pause.*) I must go back.

SAM: I know.

LEON: It was a wonderful ceremony, Sam. The beanie doesn't matter. The music, the gifts, it all doesn't matter. All the Bar Mitzvahs that I have attended had no father who loved his son as much as I have seen in this home. It was a proud moment, yes?

SAM: Yes, it was. *(Leon hugs Sam.)*

LEON: I love you, Schmooks. *(Leon salutes and exits. Sam watches his friend leave.)*

SAM: I... take care of yourself, Leon. *(Fade to black.)*

GRACE

Doug Lucie

2 Men

Gavin (40s) an American-trained English evangelist-businessman, and Lance (20s) his assistant, a zealot of the new right.

Scene: Hartstone, a home in rural England

When Lance reveals a very unpleasant aspect of his personality to Gavin, the older man threatens to fire him. Combat-trained Lance quickly responds with a threat of blackmail.

(The garden, about 9:00 p.m. Center stage is a trestle table from which dinner has been eaten. It has a white tablecloth, candelabra, and flowers as well as the remains of dinner on it. There are nine chairs around the table. Standing to one side, holding his mobile phone, is Gavin. He smokes a cigar, looking faintly upset. Lance comes on, a bit drunk, carrying a fresh bottle of brandy, which he waves in Gavin's direction with a smile. Gavin smiles back.)

LANCE: Here we are. *(He pours two brandies.)* Did you get through?

GAVIN: Yes. *(Beat.)* There's been a complication, they might have to do a Cæsearean.

LANCE: Bad news.

GAVIN: Not especially. Sophie and the baby seem quite well, so… *(Lance raises his glass.)* Cheers. *(They clink glasses.)*

LANCE: *(Indicating the table.)* They certainly know how to put on a spread.

GAVIN: What, in my school days, we'd have called a slap-up do. *(Beat.)* Is there any sign yet of Joanna?

LANCE: Funnily enough, no.

GAVIN: As if she's not in enough trouble, silly girl. She's pushing her luck, you know. Her absence at dinner was noticed. *(Beat.)*

LANCE: The noble savage hasn't been around either.

GAVIN: Freddy? You don't think…? *(Beat.)* That's all we need.

LANCE: Quite. Still, mustn't get jealous, eh? *(Slight frisson.)*

GAVIN: You're rather keen on her, aren't you?

LANCE: She's okay.

GAVIN: You should ask her out. *(Lance shrugs.)* It's about time you thought about settling down, you know. You're, what, twenty-six?

LANCE: Twenty-seven.

GAVIN: Well, there you are. The ladies won't wait forever. Settle down. Get yourself a firm loving base. *(Beat.)* Children, they're the clincher. Nothing's ever the same again once you've had children. It really is a miracle, birth. Absolute miracle. When you've seen a child being born, you can believe anything is possible; that the material world has limits that can be overcome. *(Beat.)*

LANCE: I wonder if your wife sees it that way.

GAVIN: Oh, she does. She's as happy as I am.

LANCE: No, I mean right now. Now there's a surgeon standing over her in a mask, scalpel in hand, about to slit her belly open.

GAVIN: Lance, really…

LANCE: I expect that's one miracle she could probably do without. *(Beat.)*

GAVIN: I feel bad enough already about not being there. Please…

LANCE: I've seen it done. In Nicaragua. Except it wasn't a surgeon, it was one of our guys. And it wasn't a scalpel, it was a machete. *(Beat.)*

GAVIN: What are you saying?

LANCE: I'd have thought it was pretty clear.

GAVIN: I don't believe you. *(Lance leans forward and smiles.)*

LANCE: I have photographs. *(Beat.)*

GAVIN: Are you talking about a pregnant woman?

LANCE: Yeah.

GAVIN: Dead. Alive. What?

LANCE: Half dead.

GAVIN: Half dead? Half dead is still alive.

LANCE: Not in that part of the world it isn't. *(Beat.)*

GAVIN: Is this the truth? Or are you just showing off?

LANCE: *(He smirks.)* It's the truth. *(Beat.)*

GAVIN: I've never seen this side of you before, Lance. A word of advice, let's not see it again, eh?

LANCE: *(Venomous.)* Hey… we won. Yeah? *(Beat.)* You think we did it nice? You think we walked in with a Bible and a smile? *(Beat.)* We did whatever was thought necessary. I was there! Don't pretend you don't know. Enterprise Faith was one of the Foundation's biggest backers. *(Beat.)* Sure, our boys massacred civilians when necessary, they tortured and murdered prisoners. *(Beat.)* And *we* kept the photographs. We controlled the information because that's how you win wars. *(Long pause.)*

GAVIN: I think you should pray to God…

LANCE: You don't understand, do you…?

GAVIN: Pray for forgiveness…

LANCE: It's all built on blood. Not love. *(Gavin starts to pray.)*

GAVIN: Heavenly Father, into whose care we commit our souls…

LANCE: Oh, shut it…

GAVIN: Look down with forgiveness on our unworthiness… *(Lance pulls Gavin's hands apart.)*

LANCE: Don't include me in that. Fucking hypocrite. *(Long pause as Gavin gathers himself together. He takes a sip of brandy.)*

GAVIN: I don't like to have to say this to you Lance… I had hopes for you. I thought I saw some of me in you. I'd almost come to think of you as a son. *(Beat.)* I guess I was wrong. *(Beat.)* You realize… you can't go on working for me. I've no option but to let you go. You do realize that? *(Beat.)* Well. I'm very sorry.

LANCE: No need to be.

GAVIN: There is. I made an error in judgement.

LANCE: You said it.

GAVIN: It's as much my fault as yours. I take the blame.

LANCE: Like I said, no need. *(Beat.)* Nobody's going to know any of this. You're not going to tell them. And you're not going to "let me go." Because I'm not going to tell anybody that you've been screwing Joanna. *(Beat.)* Gavin Driver, father of four, number five about to pop, the Lord's representative here on earth. Got caught with his dick in the cookie jar. *(Beat.)* But like I said, I'm not going to tell, okay?

GAVIN: Do I have your word that this will never come out?

LANCE: Yes.

GAVIN: Your *word?*

LANCE: Yes. I like this work. It suits me. Not going to queer my pitch, am I? *(Beat.)*

GAVIN: I feel I want to punch you, very hard.

LANCE: I can relate to that. It's guilt.

HAND TO HAND
Max Mayer

2 Men

Sam (50–60) a man struggling to cope with the death of his wife, and Mark (32) his son.

Scene: Here and Now

Sam and Mark have been dealing with Paula's death in their own ways. Here, Mark finally confronts his father with his feelings about his mother and the circumstances which surrounded her death.

○   ○   ○

MARK: Hi Dad.

SAM: Mark.

MARK: How've you been?

SAM: I've been kind of left in the lurch. We're supposed to be running a business together.

MARK: I know.

SAM: I called. Left a few messages.

MARK: I got them.

SAM: You got them?

MARK: Yeah.

SAM: So, why the hell didn't you call me?

MARK: I guess I didn't want to talk to you.

SAM: What do you mean?

MARK: I'm telling you the truth. I think I didn't want to talk to you because I'm tired of lying. I don't want to do that anymore, but it's very hard to tell you the truth because I'm afraid it will kill you.

SAM: What've you heard? Is it about "Mano"? They're calling the loan…

MARK: No. I haven't heard anything… Dad, I can't work at "Mano" anymore.

SAM: Mark, Maddie told me about you and Terry splitting up…

MARK: It's not about that. I don't care what kind of kitchen utensils people buy. I don't care about what we do. About the business we're in.

SAM: I asked you. I asked you before we got into this.

MARK: Yes, you did. I'm sorry.

SAM: You know what you're doing here, don't you? You're killing it. It's a little struggling calf, just getting to its feet, and you're cutting it off at the knees.

MARK: It's not a calf, it's a company. It doesn't have feelings. You don't need me anymore.

SAM: Right. I could go on five, ten, fifteen more years? For what? For you. It was all for you.

MARK: Dad, if that's true then can't you understand that I don't want it.

SAM: What'll you do?

MARK: It doesn't matter. I don't have a plan. I'll do something. I'll work for Maddie, I'll go back to school, I'll wind up on the street—

SAM: That is not a life. That is chaos.

MARK: I will not settle for your life, or Mom's.

SAM: You leave your mother out of this.

MARK: When will she be out of this, Dad? When?… You, Mom, the three of us. It's like a cage. I can't get out and nobody else can come in.

SAM: How can you talk like that? We are a family.

MARK: She left us, Dad. She left you.

SAM: She was killed. It was an accident.

MARK: No. My friend. Georgie, last year. An oncoming car jumps the median. That's an accident. Destiny. Fate. But, Mom? Still daylight. No traffic. She what… falls asleep at the wheel? A woman who took four sleeping pills before she went to bed at night?

SAM: I will not listen to anymore of this.

MARK: She left us, Dad. One car accidents are usually suicide.

SAM: That's the stupidest thing I have ever heard.

MARK: Suicide. That's what my therapist tried to tell me. That's why I left. I stayed true to Mom, to you. But, it's killing me. I am tired of mourning a mother who never existed. Of comparing every woman to a myth of perfection. Dad, I'm thirty-three years old. I can't marry. I can't leave. I can't have a family.

SAM: Was it her fault you're lazy? Was it her fault you're weak? That woman loved both of us more than you can imagine. But for you, for you the sun rose and the earth revolved.

MARK: You're still taking her side. I was a son. I needed a father. I needed a hero. And all you showed me was how to serve. How to sacrifice my life. How to kiss my mother's ass. *(Sam slaps Mark reflexively, hard, across the face. For a moment everything is still.)* Nothing for thirty-three years and then two slaps on the same day. Something is changing. Something is finally changing.

SAM: For the first moment in three years, I thank God your mother is not here.

MARK: One car accidents are usually suicide, Dad. Somewhere, she knew. Somewhere inside, she couldn't stay, either.

SAM: Get out of my house. You told me what you wanted to tell me, now, get out of my house.

MARK: If it would have kept her alive, I would have let her slap me till her palms bled. I don't want to die by accident. I don't want to live my life by accidents.

SAM: You cannot imagine. Maybe, when you have a child...My grandfather beat my father. Nearly every night. He told me stories. He vowed he would never lay a hand on any of us. And he never did. The day you were born I made the same promise to your mother...

MARK: Dad.

SAM: Please, leave now. I want to be by myself.

MARK: Dad, you're released. All promises are null and void. All debts paid.

SAM: Get out.

THE HARRY AND SAM DIALOGUES

Karen Ellison

2 Men

Harry and Sam (30-40), a couple of regular guys.

Scene: Here and Now

Harry and Sam have been best friends for 20 years. Here, they engage in idle, yet imaginative, banter while shooting pool.

O   O   O

(Fade in. McDougal's Bar, Harry and Sam's hangout. Harry and Sam play pool. Two stools sit nearby.)

HARRY: Say ya' gotta tree.

SAM: I gotta tree.

HARRY: Ya' gotta whole forest 'a trees.

SAM: I gotta whole forest 'a trees.

HARRY: Now say there's only one person for miles around—a guy with one of those red and black jackets and a ski hat with an axe…

SAM: A lumberjack.

HARRY: Whatever. And he's chopping one 'a your trees. But he only chopped part way.

SAM: Gotcha.

HARRY: Now he's pulling out his lunch pail.

SAM: A red one?

HARRY: Yeah.

SAM: Like yours?

HARRY: Yeah.

SAM: (*Fondly.*) With the matching thermos?

HARRY: Yeah! Okay! And he's starting to eat.

SAM: Lunch.

HARRY: Yeah. So this guy—this tree chopper—while he's eating his lunch, he gets a call on his beeper.

SAM: He gotta beeper?

HARRY: Yeah.

SAM: This lumberjack, in the middle 'a the woods using an ax to chop a tree, has a beeper.

HARRY: Yeah, he has a beeper! He's part of a large tree chopping corporation.

SAM: Timber mill.

HARRY: Whatever. So this guy gets a call on his beeper. He pulls out his cellular phone— (*Harry gives Sam a look.*) 'cause there's no phone booth in the woods...

SAM: 'Course.

HARRY: ...And he calls the number that flashed on his beeper, and the guy on the other end says, "Come on over to the plant, quick! Your wife's having a baby!"

SAM: At the plant?

HARRY: No, not at the plant. At the hospital!

SAM: The lumberjack—he know about this?

HARRY: What?

SAM: He know his wife's gonna have a baby?

HARRY: Yeah! 'Course he knows!

SAM: 'Cause the way you said in, "Come on over, Your wife's having a baby," sounds like it's a surprise.

HARRY: 'Course he knows about it. He whaddaya'-call-it—helped!

SAM: He knew she was pregnant?

HARRY: Yeah, Sam. He knew she was pregnant.

SAM: She wasn't keeping it from him?

HARRY: She's as big as a house, for Christ's sake!

SAM: Don't curse. He hasn't maybe been out of town for nine months chopping trees in the... Black Forest, say?

HARRY: No! He works about fifteen miles from home.

SAM: Fifteen miles.

HARRY: Yeah. (*Sam writes something down. Harry looks over his shoulder.*)

SAM: What's his wife's name?

HARRY: Doesn't matter what his wife's name is!

SAM: Just thought it might be important.

HARRY: It isn't. Trust me. So, anyway, this tree chopper puts down his lunch...

SAM: What's he eating?

HARRY: What?

SAM: What's he eating for lunch?

HARRY: It doesn't matter what he's eating for lunch.

SAM: How do I know? How do I know it doesn't matter? What if you're going to ask me the contents of his stomach when they pump it during the autopsy after his car is pushed off a cliff by an eighteen wheeler driven by Yahn and Eric, the perpetrators of the tax fraud that the young lumberjack, Yorn von Yorn, was going to expose at Shady Pines, the timber mill where he works? It could be important! Everything's important to me now, Harry, because I don't know, do I? And sure. Sure you'll say, "Trust me." Trust you? Like the time you were telling that joke to the lodge about the porpoise and the prostitute, only you left out that part about...

HARRY: Salad.

SAM: Salad?

HARRY: He's eating salad for lunch, and then the tree chopper runs to his pickup truck and drives off to his wife whose name doesn't matter who's having a baby at the hospital.

SAM: Natural or cesarean?

HARRY: How should I know what kind salad it was? So, anyway, while the tree chopper is at the hospital, this one tree that he chopped part way, remember?

SAM: I remember.

HARRY: 'Cause it was sometime ago that I mentioned that.

SAM: I remember.

HARRY: This one tree falls down.

SAM: Lawsuit!

HARRY: No lawsuit!

SAM: It lands on someone's car!

HARRY: Who's telling this story? No. There's nothing and no one around for miles. Just trees.

SAM: Trees.

HARRY: Trees. So?

SAM: So?

HARRY: When the tree hits the ground, does it make any kind 'a noise?

SAM: Let me get this straight: if a tree falls in the forest, and no one's there to hear it, does it make a sound?

HARRY: Well... yeah. That's another way to say it.

SAM: No.

HARRY: What?

SAM: No. (*Indicating pool table.*) It's your shot. (*Harry puts his hand to his back.*) You okay?

HARRY: Had to sleep on the end of the bed. Ya' don't want time to think about it?

SAM: No. She made ya' do that? Ballbuster.

HARRY: I'll give ya' a couple minutes.

SAM: Don't need time. The answer is still no.

HARRY: No, huh?

SAM: No.

HARRY: Ya' don't want to ask me some questions?

SAM: No.

HARRY: Like are there any animals in the forest?

SAM: No.

HARRY: Maybe ya' want to ask me what's on the ground in the forest?

SAM: No.

HARRY: Grass?

SAM: No.

HARRY: Dirt?

SAM: No.

HARRY: Moss?

SAM: No.

HARRY: Moose goo?

SAM: No.

HARRY: No sound?

SAM: No sound. (*Pause.*)

HARRY: Well, this really stinks. I mean this eats it. You're not play-ing along!

SAM: Ya' asked me a question, I answered. (*Smug.*) Go ahead. Ask me another. (*Pause.*)

HARRY: Okay. It's the beginning of time, and there's this big red barn owned by Caveman Farmer Wilson...

SAM: Cut to the chase.

HARRY: Okay. Whi...

SAM: The egg. (*Pause. The following exchange takes place fast and furious.*)

HARRY: Is there life after death?

SAM: No.

HARRY: Who built the pyramids?

SAM: Martians.

HARRY: What is Stonehedge?

SAM: Primitive wristwatch — made by Martians.

HARRY: Why can't ya' get a good five cent cigar?

SAM: Recession.

HARRY: What do vice presidents do?

SAM: Wait for someone to die.

HARRY: What is Bigfoot?

SAM: Giant gorilla-man from Mars.

HARRY: Where is Jimmy Hoffa?

SAM: Yankee Stadium, left field, seats 3A through D.

(*Fade out.*)

THE LAST INTIMACY

Jean Reynolds

2 Men

Weaver (35) a somewhat unbalanced man, and Claude (40s) his brother.

Scene: A funeral home, 1950

Weaver and Claude have inherited their father's funeral home and made it into a family business. Unknown to Claude, Weaver has brought Selene, a woman of questionable virtue and background, home from a local gin mill. Here, Weaver greets Claude in the morning when he arrives at the home and breaks the news to him about Selene.

○   ○   ○

CLAUDE: When Pop said take care of you, I didn't think he meant this.

WEAVER: *(Startled.)* Pop said that? Pop said take care of me?

CLAUDE: Yes.

WEAVER: I didn't know Pop said that.

CLAUDE: Pop said take care of you.

WEAVER: I didn't know Pop thought about me.

CLAUDE: Of course Pop thought about you.

WEAVER: Why didn't Pop tell me he thought about me?

CLAUDE: Maybe he forgot.

WEAVER: He forgot?

CLAUDE: Weaver, I don't know.

WEAVER: I wish I could be like you.

CLAUDE: Like me?

WEAVER: You're at ease in the world. Things make sense to you. You see clearly. How could Pop teach you to see clearly and teach me—?

CLAUDE: He taught you your side of the business.

WEAVER: I didn't want to know.

CLAUDE: That's what he taught you. He taught you what he knew.

WEAVER: He taught me.

CLAUDE: It's a father's job.

WEAVER: Why did Pop get married?

CLAUDE: He wanted a family.

WEAVER: I asked him why he had us. He said you don't think about why when you're making babies.

CLAUDE: He wanted sons to run the business.

WEAVER: If he liked so many women, he shouldn't have gotten married.

CLAUDE: One woman isn't enough.

WEAVER: The right woman would be enough. *(Selene relaxes in Weaver's room. She finds a bathrobe, removes her dress, and changes into the bathrobe.)*

CLAUDE: It's the way men are. The way Pop was. The way I am. The way you are.

WEAVER: No.

CLAUDE: One woman is too final.

WEAVER: No.

CLAUDE: C'mon, Weaver.

WEAVER: The right woman would be enough.

CLAUDE: Every time you meet a woman you think she's the right woman.

WEAVER: I went to Kelly's last night. I had a few drinks at Kelly's.

CLAUDE: By yourself?

WEAVER: Kelly's was crowded.

CLAUDE: So you had a few drinks with the crowd?

WEAVER: I had a few drinks with a beautiful woman.

CLAUDE: Ah.

WEAVER: Ah?

CLAUDE: Just ah.

WEAVER: Oh.

CLAUDE: Then what? What did you do after you had a few drinks with a beautiful woman?

WEAVER: Had more drinks.

CLAUDE: Then what?

WEAVER: Then I came home.

CLAUDE: Ah. *(Beat.)* With the skirt?

WEAVER: Skirt? What skirt?

CLAUDE: You know what skirt.

WEAVER: I didn't come home with a skirt.

CLAUDE: Don't lie to me, Weaver.

WEAVER: She's not a skirt.

CLAUDE: Did you bring her in here?

WEAVER: Yes.

CLAUDE: I don't want them in here! Take them upstairs. We talked about this, Weaver. You promised.

WEAVER: She wanted to see—

CLAUDE: See what?!

WEAVER: You know.

CLAUDE: What?

WEAVER: Oh, you know.

CLAUDE: No, I don't know.

WEAVER: Everything.

CLAUDE: Hell, I'm not against a good time.

WEAVER: Like the old man.

CLAUDE: Just don't have it in here.

WEAVER: You're like the old man, Claude.

CLAUDE: Me?

WEAVER: The way you treat Ellen—

CLAUDE: What's wrong with the way I treat Ellen? I don't want to talk about the way I treat Ellen. I don't bring trash home! I don't bring trash in here!

WEAVER: She's not trash!

CLAUDE: Go to a hotel!

WEAVER: She's not trash!

CLAUDE: Control yourself.

WEAVER: Like you do?

CLAUDE: I don't have anything to do with the skirts at Kelly's.

WEAVER: You go to another town.

CLAUDE: That's right, Weaver. I go where no one knows me. For a little fun. I run this business practically by myself. I do it all. I need to get away. I need to forget. I need some fun, okay?

WEAVER: Just like the old man—

CLAUDE: I don't want to talk about it.

WEAVER: He brought women here.

CLAUDE: He did not! *(Beat.)* Well, maybe he did. That doesn't mean you have to.

WEAVER: What I do is *my* business.

CLAUDE: Not when it affects *our* business. When it affects *our* business then it is *my* business as well as *your* business.

WEAVER: Claude, I want someone to help.

CLAUDE: What?

WEAVER: I don't mean to help with *them*.

CLAUDE: Help?

WEAVER: Someone to help.

CLAUDE: Help what?

WEAVER: Help me.

CLAUDE: Help you what?

WEAVER: Just help, you know.

CLAUDE: You don't need—

WEAVER: An assistant?

CLAUDE: An assistant?!

WEAVER: An assistant.

CLAUDE: What for?

WEAVER: To assist.

CLAUDE: You don't need an assistant. You do your work and I take care of everything else. Pop didn't have an assistant. Pop did your work and my work and he didn't have an assistant.

WEAVER: Someone to—

CLAUDE: I make those decisions.

WEAVER: Someone to help.

CLAUDE: You're incapable of making sensible decisions.

WEAVER: No, I'm not.

CLAUDE: You want to run the business?

WEAVER: No, no.

CLAUDE: All right.

WEAVER: I can make sensible decisions.

CLAUDE: You want to run the business?

WEAVER: No, no. But I want someone to help.

CLAUDE: Finished downstairs? Everything taken care of?

WEAVER: Everything.

CLAUDE: Work done?

WEAVER: Done.

CLAUDE: Done already?

WEAVER: Already done.

CLAUDE: Then you don't need someone to help!

WEAVER: I told you I don't need help with *them*. I need someone to help me. With my thoughts. To organize, sort, put in order, you know.

CLAUDE: Stop it, Weaver!

WEAVER: I can't stop it!

CLAUDE: You've got to settle down. Ellen says—and I think she's right—get responsible. Get married.

WEAVER: Get married?

CLAUDE: Have kids. Be like everybody else. Why don't you meet a nice girl?

WEAVER: Last time I met a nice girl, you married her.

CLAUDE: That was ten years ago, Weaver. Get over it.

WEAVER: I'm over it.

CLAUDE: If you settle down, well, then you'd settle down, lead a normal life.

WEAVER: I'd like to lead a normal life, but my thoughts—

CLAUDE: Stop thinking!

WEAVER: It would be a relief.

CLAUDE: To me too.

WEAVER: To settle down.

CLAUDE: A big relief.

WEAVER: To be an average man.

CLAUDE: Work on it, Weaver, work on it.

WEAVER: I'm working on it, Claude, I'm working on it.

CLAUDE: Good.

WEAVER: That's what I wanted to tell you. Someone's working on it with me. She's upstairs.

CLAUDE: Who's upstairs?

WEAVER: The woman I had a few drinks with last night.

CLAUDE: The skirt is still here?

WEAVER: I told you, she's not a skirt!

CLAUDE: What the hell is she doing here?

WEAVER: She—

CLAUDE: I'll get rid of the skirt.

WEAVER: Stop calling her a skirt!

CLAUDE: I know the kind of woman who hangs out in Kelly's.

WEAVER: She's different.

CLAUDE: Different?

WEAVER: Different!

CLAUDE: Different?! They're all the same. All the same.

WEAVER: No, Claude.

CLAUDE: This one's different, huh?

WEAVER: You'll see.

CLAUDE: In what way?

WEAVER: You'll see.

CLAUDE: In what way is she different?

WEAVER: She has the mark. The mark that marks her for me.

CLAUDE: Don't talk like that. It gives me the creeps.

WEAVER: I can't explain, Claude, because you don't understand. Because you don't believe in magic.

CLAUDE: No, I don't.

WEAVER: You have no vision.

CLAUDE: I suppose you have vision?

WEAVER: I'm talking about intangibles.

CLAUDE: Weaver—

WEAVER: I'm talking about things you can't measure. I'm talking about things you can't add up.

CLAUDE: I don't have time for vision!

WEAVER: After you meet her... well, I was going to tell you this after you meet her, but... well, I... I—

CLAUDE: What?!

WEAVER: Once you *see* her, you'll know... you'll know she belongs here.

CLAUDE: Weaver.

WEAVER: I... I—

CLAUDE: Finish your thought.

WEAVER: I offered her… I offered her a job.

CLAUDE: A what?

WEAVER: A job.

CLAUDE: You can't offer her a job.

WEAVER: Why not?

CLAUDE: Because you can't offer her a job, that's why not.

WEAVER: I did. I asked her to help.

CLAUDE: You should have asked me.

WEAVER: You want to help me?

CLAUDE: I do help you. *(Heading toward Weaver's room.)* I'll get rid of her.

WEAVER: No.

CLAUDE: Hey, I might even have some fun—

WEAVER: No!

CLAUDE: —before I throw her out.

WEAVER: No, Claude!

CLAUDE: Hey, as long as she's here—

WEAVER: Not her.

CLAUDE: I might as well.

WEAVER: Leave her alone.

CLAUDE: You objecting?

WEAVER: Yes, I'm objecting.

CLAUDE: Hey, Weaver. *(Selene, hearing argument, exits Weaver's room, walks toward bereavement room.)*

WEAVER: If you touch her, I'll… I'll get a gun!

CLAUDE: Hey, calm down.

WEAVER: I can get a gun! You'd be surprised!

CLAUDE: All right, Weaver, calm down.

WEAVER: I'll kill you! That's what I'll do!

CLAUDE: Weaver—

WEAVER: I'LL KILL YOU.

CLAUDE: WEAVER—

WEAVER: I'll kill you! I swear I'll kill you! She's mine! Mine!

CLAUDE: Okay, Weaver.

WEAVER: Mine.

CLAUDE: All right. All right.

WEAVER: You'll see.

MURMURING JUDGES

David Hare

2 Men
  Beckett (50s) a prison guard, and Gerard (20s) a prisoner.

Scene: A prison in England

Gerard has been sentenced to five years in prison for something he didn't do. Here, the fearful young Irishman is processed by Beckett.

O   O   O

(The stage darkens and we move into the enormous, gloomy space of the prison reception area. The prison is Victorian, with a gigantic door just discernible at the back. It is late night, with only a few high lights making shapes through the gloom. What by day is a busy area with a very long desk running along one side is now deserted and quiet. Raymond Beckett, in his fifties, large, balding, with a big stomach beneath his blue pullover, and an open, blunt manner, is waiting behind the desk. At once from the back Gerard is escorted out of the darkness by a short, foxy-looking officer who brings him in to face Beckett.)

BECKETT: Strip off.

GERARD: I'm sorry.

BECKETT: Empty all your pockets and take off your clothes. *(Gerard looks, a little bewildered, around the huge space. The other officer has already disappeared into the darkness at the other side of the area.)*

GERARD: Here? *(Beckett looks up from the admission sheets, catching Gerard's tone.)*

BECKETT: Don't you know the procedures? Haven't you been in prison before?

GERARD: No.

BECKETT: Weren't you on remand?

GERARD: I was on bail.

BECKETT: So is this your first time? *(Gerard looks at him, not need-ing to answer. Beckett seems to show a sudden sympathy. The other officer has returned with a large cloth bag.)* Why aren't you emptying your pockets? *(Gerard moves to the desk and empties his pockets on it. Beckett has a plastic bag, which he puts the stuff in.)*

Here. Your things will go in this bag. *(Gerard starts to undress. The silent officer has started to empty what looks like a pile of rags onto a table opposite.)*

BECKETT: Why are you so late?

GERARD: They took me to Pentonville. But then it turned out there wasn't any room.

BECKETT: There's no room here. But we'll make some. Why is it midnight?

GERARD: Then there wasn't a van.

BECKETT: Again?

GERARD: They couldn't find one.

BECKETT: Have you eaten?

GERARD: I had some spaghetti. But then I lost it.

BECKETT: How are you feeling?

GERARD: Not very well. *(Beckett is filling out forms. The other offi-cer, noncommittal, now goes to lean against a desk a long way off. He lights a cigarette, says nothing, just watches.)*

BECKETT: We've put you on D-wing. We shouldn't really. It's for lif-ers. But it's that or sleeping in the chapel. *(There is a sudden si-lence. Gerard is in the middle of the area, covering his nakedness with his hand. His clothes are in a pile beside him. Beckett holds out the form on a clipboard to the naked man.)* Sign here.

GERARD: I can't. You've taken my pen. *(Beckett looks at him a mo-ment, not sure if Gerard is taking a piss. Gerard signs.)*

BECKETT: Would you like a cigarette?

GERARD: No, thank you.

BECKETT: You're meant to have a shower. But the water's off. So you can get dressed.

GERARD: I'm sorry?

BECKETT: There's clothes over there. *(He points toward the heap. Gerard goes over and collects his prison clothes.)*
Gerard McKinnon.

GERARD: Yes.

BECKETT: I'm giving you a number. All right? A6324. That's what you'll answer to. Do you need to hear it again?

GERARD: No, I've got it.

BECKETT: The governor will come and see you in the morning. And we'll fix you with a job. Prison isn't just sitting around.

GERARD: No. *(He is frowning at the outsize tops and trousers, while at the same time trying to stay decent.)* No, I know that.

BECKETT: You'll see all the departments. There's a reception committee. Probation, medical, educational, the chaplain. They'll advise you on how to survive the jail.

GERARD: Survive?

BECKETT: Just so you don't waste your time. It's up to you. You can make this place work for you. Anyone can. It's not hard. Get educated. Be sensible.

GERARD: Yes. *(He stops a moment, hesitating to speak, halfway dressed.)* It's silly, you see, I was sent down with two other people. I was expecting they'd be here with me.

BECKETT: That's not the policy.

GERARD: No. I'm not complaining. I don't like them that much. It's just... they're more experienced. So I thought they might sort of see me through.

BECKETT: Yeah. *(He is looking hard at Gerard.)* Look, I think someone better tell you. Before you get started. You'd better learn. I've seen people go crazy when it's their first time. *(He pauses.)* What you have to do is put the past behind you. Do you understand? *(Gerard frowns for a moment as he dresses.)* You got done. You did wrong. Society's put you in jail. Okay, now don't brood. Work to the future. Work to the moment when you get out.

GERARD: Yes, I see.

BECKETT: Because you know what's most dangerous?

GERARD: No, I don't.

BECKETT: The worst is getting bitter. That's the thing. I watch it. That's the thing that messes people up. Do you see? If you get an attitude. If you get an attitude, I tell you, it's worse than catching the clap. *(He suddenly raises his voice across the area, without warning.)* An attitude's the clap. Do you understand me?

GERARD: What sort of attitude?

BECKETT: If you start thinking, they done me wrong. I'm always in the right, I hate this place, I shouldn't be here, and, pardon my French, sod you all, if you think that, then it kills you. You're finished. It burns you up.

GERARD: Yes. *(He looks at Beckett nervously.)* I'll tell you what worries me.

BECKETT: Yes?

GERARD: I got a wife.

BECKETT: Okay.

GERARD: She's not my wife actually. But we have two children. One of them has Down's.

BECKETT: Yes. Go on.

GERARD: Down's syndrome, you see. *(He pauses, emotion about to overwhelm him for a moment.)* And now I'm not sure how they'll keep their head's above water. *(He stands a moment, the clothes ridiculously big for him.)*

BECKETT: Right, well that's it, that's what I'm saying. There's some people here going to help you with that. There's people with degrees from Oxford University. They're giving up their lives to help you adjust. So you can live without being banged up. *(He gets up now to go and pick up the old clothes which Gerard has discarded on the floor, and to put them in a bag.)* It's a long job. It's not always easy. It's not like changing your clothes. *(Beckett is now standing directly opposite Gerard. His original clothes are in a plastic bag, while he is like Charlie Chaplin, his trousers puddling around his feet, his jacket swamping him.)*

GERARD: Do you have a belt?

BECKETT: You're not allowed a belt. You'll kill yourself. *(He nods a moment.)* Do you want a cup of tea?

GERARD: I won't, thank you. *(There's a moment's pause, things oddly formal and polite.)* I'd like to sleep.

BECKETT: Good. You look good.

GERARD: Thank you. *(Beckett looks to the other officer.)*

BECKETT: Shall we go up?

PERPETUAL CARE

Jocelyn Beard

2 Men
 James (60–70) a man at the end of his life, and a Demon (30–40)

Scene: A cemetery

The Demon has been sent to earth to observe the death of James Delacroix. In human guise, the Demon rents a room from James and the two have become quite friendly. Here, the Demon keeps the older man company on a visit to his wife's grave. When the two embark on a discussion of the dangers of life in the late twentieth century, the Demon reveals more of himself than he had intended.

O   O   O

(James and the Demon tend to Lottie Lemon's grave. The Demon is down on his knees pulling weeds while James leans against the stone.)

JAMES: ...yes sir, didn't have no trouble round here until Packy Winston up and died. He's over there now, next to that big stone, right next to the two angels, see? Old Packy kept things nice and neat. You see what it say right there? *(Indicating a spot on Lottie's gravestone.)* Perpetual Care. That means as long as this bone yard is takin' customers that someone's gotta keep little Lottie Lemon's grave presentable. You try explaining that to Chuck—he's the maintenance man—his idea of perpetual care is to do a little rakin' in between beers. He steals the flowers, too. Gives 'em to his gal. That's why I plant Emma Mae's right in the earth with her. *(The Demon rises and scans the inscription on Lottie's stone.)*

DEMON: Carlotta Lemon. Born October 10, 1927. Died December 24, 1937.

JAMES: Worst Christmas there ever was. The Lemon's lived in that old gray house over there. *(Points.)* Just at the end of May

Street. Lottie and me were great friends, you see. We used to sit in Sunday School together. Coupla cutups. Miss Hamilton used to say: "Carlotta Lemon and James Delacroix! You are one pair that Noah would have banned from the Ark!" *(The Demon smiles despite himself.)* Yessir, Christmas nineteen hundred and twenty-seven. Lottie and I were going to be in the church pageant together. She was Mary and I was... *(James pauses and smiles sadly, this is the first time he's thought of this in many years.)* ...I was the innkeeper that turned them away. We rehearsed for weeks and weeks, seems like. Everyone in the neighborhood was so excited that Lottie was gonna be Mary and hold the little baby Jesus. *(James pauses, lost in thought.)*

DEMON: What happened?

JAMES: *(Plainly.)* She was hit by a truck.

DEMON: A truck?

JAMES: Running across Mulberry to get to the church. She was so excited, I guess she forgot to look. *(The Demon silently regards the grave.)*

JAMES: Worst Christmas ever.

DEMON: *(In an effort to break the mood.)* But surely there have been happy ones since.

JAMES: The finest any man could have hoped for.

DEMON: I've always been puzzled by the nostalgic attachment that mortals have for the birth of...

JAMES: *(Laughing.)* Mortals? Where're you from, son, outer space? *(The Demon realizes his tiny slip.)* I guess you must be, because you can actually have a conversation with that grandson of mine. What's that name he calls himself?

DEMON: Mello D.

JAMES: Mello D. You tell me, what kind of name is that: deaf, dope or stupid?

DEMON: *(With a smile.)* I rather think it's all three.

JAMES: That must be the problem with "David," then. It's none of the above. It's just... David.

DEMON: David is a fine name.

JAMES: It was her father's. Emma Mae's. David Brown. Now there was a mortal for you. I'll never forget the day that Uncle Jasper's Ford broke down in front of David Brown's little farm in North Carolina. It was just after the war…

DEMON: War?

JAMES: Two. It was just after World War II, and Uncle Jasper promised me $150 for driving his old Ford from here to his new home in Tampa, Florida. Well, the stupid thing ate oil for breakfast but old Jasper, he never bothered to mention it. So there I was, on the most beautiful day in God's book, marching right up the walk to David Brown's front door.

DEMON: And Emma Mae opened that door.

JAMES: *(Vaguely surprised.)* That's right.

DEMON: She must have been lovely, James.

JAMES: *(Reflecting.)* Lovely. Now there's a word. Lovely. Not beautiful or pretty—because Emma Mae wasn't either of those. She was… so much more than those. She was lovely. The most lovely girl I'd ever seen… standing there with that look…

DEMON: Like she'd been waiting for you.

JAMES: *(Giving the Demon a close look.)* You're pretty smart for a guy who doesn't have anything better to do than to help an old man tend to his wife's grave.

DEMON: I didn't mean…

JAMES: She'd been waiting for me, all right. In her mind she was packed and ready to go, but it took me another six months to convince old David Brown to let me take away his only daughter. He was a man who could do anything. Maybe he could have talked some sense into Davey.

DEMON: The boy is young.

JAMES: True, but in case you haven't noticed, this world's not as understanding of youth as it used to be. When you were a kid, did your momma hafta worry about you smokin' crack down to the corner?

DEMON: The corner?

JAMES: No sir, she did not. She didn't hafta worry 'bout crack or crank. No gangs, no AIDS, no skinheads. Nothin'. *(The Demon stares at James for a moment. He is being seized by memories of his earthly life. These are things which he has not been able to contemplate for a very, very long time.)*

DEMON: When I was a boy. It was so very long ago, you see. So very long ago. The things I've done... When I was a boy, James, it is true: there were no corners that tempted with belladonnas. There was, however, a plague. Like yours. Worse in effect, though, for we had no hospice or 1-800 hotline. No caring doctors or treatments. Just death. A death unlike any you can imagine, James Delacroix. A burning blackness that swallowed up half the world. *(Softly, amending.)* Half my world. And with the Plague came the gangs, like yours, though again worse in effect. These gangs preyed upon the dead as well as the living. These gangs roved the land devouring what little spirit remained. One such gang came to my door. My father had been missing for weeks. He had ridden off to find a... physician, for my mother had fallen ill. None of the servants would touch her. Most fled into the countryside. Who could cast blame upon their miserable souls? Not I, James, for I have done worse than to desert a dying mistress. My sister, Aurore, tended to our mother and herself became ill. I was just a boy, like David, and could do nothing to help. And then... and then, murder walked through our door on big, ugly peasant feet. A gang of men and women who had been looting their way through our valley walked into our courtyard just as my mother gasped her last breath. Their leader tore pearls from her blackened neck while my sister tried weakly to fight him off. His women tore the silk from my mother's body as the men took Aurore. When they had finished with her they slit her throat and laughed as she staggered to the little altar in my mother's chamber. Aurore died on that altar, begging His mercy. And then the women tore the bloodied silk from her body. They took everything that their savage little band could carry, and then, just before they left, their leader came for me. *(There is a moment of silence.)* So you see, James, time has not changed the world overly much.

STEPHEN AND MR. WILDE
Jim Bartley

2 Men
  Oscar Wilde (27) British dramatist, and Stephen (30s) his black
manservant.

Scene: Toronto, 1882

Wilde has hired Stephen to accompany him on his lecture tour of
North America. While visiting Toronto, a newspaper reporter confides
to Wilde that he suspects that Stephen is, in fact, wanted for the murder of a former slave owner in Baltimore. This manages to raise a small
bit of doubt in Wilde's mind about the character of his valet, who is, in
fact, a former slave. Wilde uses this doubt to start a dialogue with
Stephen about the facts of life, and he finds himself beginning to understand the other man's life.

○   ○   ○

*(Wilde's suite: later that evening. Stephen is reading a book.
Wilde enters, returning from his lecture.)*
WILDE: God! *(Stephen ignores him.)* What a ghastly evening!
  *(Wilde removes his cape, goes to the table and pours himself a
  whiskey. Stephen turns a page of his book. Wilde savors his first
  sip.)* Do you wish to hear about it?
STEPHEN: *(Head in book.)* You know I do, sir.
WILDE: Yes, well that Hawthorne fellow… he's a tawdry piece of
  business. Told me I misquoted Pope. Then he started spewing
  Ruskin at me. I've had *tea* with Ruskin. I came back at him with
  Walter Pater, a little Swinburne… but the man's done a fair bit
  of reading, quite nearly had me by the throat for a brief moment. Of course he stayed up the whole night memorizing pas-
  sages like any schoolboy just so he could dangle them in my
  face. And *smirking* at me the whole time.
STEPHEN: Why do you dine with these men?
WILDE: I long… to *convert* them. They could be poets some of

them, dramatists… Everything is a story to them. All they lack is human sympathy. Besides, if I manage to charm them they will write favorably of me. It's a sort of vanity game. Never become popular, Stephen. It turns one into a kind of whore.

STEPHEN: We all sell ourselves in some degree.

WILDE: *(Eyeing him.)* We're going to be terse and cynical tonight are we? *(Moves away.)* Oh, and the *lecture*… Hawthorne sat in the front row and scribbled nonstop, feverishly in fact. Then he'd stare at me with those hard little eyes—like a buzzard eyeing a piece of carrion. *(Realizing what he's said.)* He's obviously blind. *(He reclines on the couch, watching Stephen.)* What are you reading?

STEPHEN: The Bible.

WILDE: Is it yours?

STEPHEN: Found it in the desk over there.

WILDE: Planted by the Temperance Union. *(He drinks.)* What is Sweet Jesus up to? Any miracles?

STEPHEN: He hasn't been born yet.

WILDE: Well, I shan't spoil it for you. But the plot improves toward the end. *(Pause.)* Do you believe in the Christian god?

STEPHEN: Don't know why I should, sir.

WILDE: Mmmm. He hasn't been overly generous with you has he, I mean your people. But then his hands are tied really. It's that damned original sin—everything's *our* fault. *(Pause.)* Did you stumble across the bawdy house?

STEPHEN: *(Setting bible aside.)* Several, sir.

WILDE: Oh, excellent. Which do you recommend?

STEPHEN: The least conspicuous.

WILDE: Of course. Is it far? It would be safer to walk wouldn't it, rather than hire a cab? No witnesses.

STEPHEN: Unless you're followed.

WILDE: We shan't be followed this time of night.

STEPHEN: *We?* I think I'll stay here if you don't mind.

WILDE: I do mind. It's much better with two, we can compare notes afterward. *(Silence.)* Of course if you'd rather mope about here and brood over those revolutionary pamphlets of yours…

STEPHEN: Pamphlets?

WILDE: The ones badly hidden in the lining of your jacket. *(Stephen looks at him.)* All about brotherhood and defending the race. But surely you've read them dozens of times by now.

STEPHEN: Did you search through my jacket?

WILDE: Certainly not. The lining is torn. I moved your jacket from the couch this afternoon and they fell out upon the floor. *(Beat.)* You don't believe me. I must say you're fortunate they didn't fall out upon another floor, among less generous company.

STEPHEN: Where have you put them.

WILDE: Safely in your room. I confess I've borrowed one.

STEPHEN: Why.

WILDE: Simply… to consider it—and my own response to it. I feel I've learned something about you. Something you needn't have kept from me.

STEPHEN: It's not your concern sir.

WILDE: Perhaps not. Provided of course you don't murder me in my sleep, or run off before your contract is expired… I'd consider it a loss either way.

STEPHEN: Do you think I could do that? Murder you?

WILDE: I should think less of you if you did. Stephen. I'm jesting.

STEPHEN: Yes sir, always jesting.

WILDE: *(Firm.)* And you are too serious. *(Gentler.)* Most discussions are improved by a sense of irony. You do tend to forget that sometimes, with your moods.

STEPHEN: Every time I disagree with you, you call it a mood. Has it occurred to you, sir, that I see things different from you?

WILDE: Clearly you do.

STEPHEN: Those pamphlets concern my people, how to lift ourselves up. You'll just feel threatened by them like white man.

WILDE: But I am not every white man. You know I'm sympathetic.

STEPHEN: How do I know that? When you turn everything we talk about into a joke. What did you think when you read them?

WILDE: They do seem… a trifle radical.

STEPHEN: You see? Why I hid them? You picture me with a knife between my teeth, sneaking into your bedroom in the wee hours—

WILDE: Dear god, Stephen, you *numbskull* that was a joke!

STEPHEN: When a man jokes about death, it shows his fear.

WILDE: Yes, I do think you're right—but not in this case. I understand the need to rebel, among an oppressed people. Your pamphlets are very... inspiring.

STEPHEN: They spread good ideas. Ideas that give my people dignity.

WILDE: Anything against bedding a white woman?

STEPHEN: Yes, in fact.

WILDE: *(Losing patience.)* Pah, what nonsense. Is whiteness contagious? *(Pause.)* Stephen... god, I hate it when we argue. It's the distrust. And this need you feel to *hide* yourself from me... why do you feel that? *(Pause.)* Will you come out with me? Let us be friends tonight. Not master, not servant. Just friends.

STEPHEN: Are you sure we can be friends, sir, in the usual sense?

WILDE: We can try an *un*usual sense.

STEPHEN: But how might I address you, if I'm your friend.

WILDE: Address me? Call me Oscar. *(Pause.)* Doesn't seem quite right does it.

STEPHEN: Do you pay your friends to wash your collars and run errands for you?

WILDE: Stephen if you're unhappy with your work, or your wages...

STEPHEN: No, you miss the point. I can be your friend tonight, but tomorrow I'll still be doing your laundry. We can't pretend to be equals.

WILDE: *(After a moment.)* Now I feel so dreadfully guilty.

STEPHEN: I don't mean you to, sir. *(A doubt.)* I don't think.

WILDE: Well you've done it now. I feel quite the slave driver.

STEPHEN: You're far from that, believe me.

WILDE: Well I try to be fair. *(A touch of sarcasm.)* I mean I know there are *insurmountable* class barriers... but it's *you* who have missed the point. As long as this wretched tour continues you *are* my only friend. And I yours. We're stuck with each other. *(Pause.)* I'm fond of you. You're intelligent, gentle, attractive... Now will you join me? Or will you insist on staying here and boiling my underwear.

STEPHEN: A good servant would do that.

WILDE: A friend would come with me.

STEPHEN: Sir… I don't go to whorehouses. I don't enjoy a place like that. Maybe I am a little… antediluvian.

WILDE: But didn't the Army teach you to chase women? You *were* in the Union army…

STEPHEN: I've told you sir I don't know how many times, the army freed me from bondage. They taught me to fight, to read—

WILDE: Yes, I remember, but surely they taught you to whore about and to drink, it's a military tradition.

STEPHEN: I drank a fair amount. Liquor alters a man's judgement, not to mention his liver.

WILDE: Well I'll allow your eccentric stand on drink, but to give up the sexual act is sheer moral depravity.

STEPHEN: *(Looks at him.)* You know what it is—your wit? You just say the opposite of what people expect. People say it's good to abstain from drink, you say it's a sign of corruption. Or you just smash idols, make fun of Jesus, of the Bible… It's just… impudence.

WILDE: Stephen, please. The essence of wit is its *form,* its *nuance.* To describe only the content commits a grave injustice. Besides, it's involuntary. I can't help it. I want you to like me.

STEPHEN: But there's no need. I don't dislike you, sir.

WILDE: That sounds rather equivocal.

STEPHEN: Well then, I do like you… well enough. Most of the time.

WILDE: *(Gratified, careful not to show it.)* Splendid. Then the class barrier is not impenetrable. Shall we go?

STEPHEN: White whores don't sleep with Negroes.

WILDE: Nonsense. Dark flesh is a novelty. The get bored you know.

STEPHEN: *(After a judicious moment.)* Yes, I'll go with you.

WILDE: Good fellow!

STEPHEN: For your sake. You're better not alone in a place like that.

WILDE: And drunk as a sailor you mean. Never mind, save me from the cutthroats, I shall be honored. *(A bit too effusive.)* But you wait till the ladies see you. They'll stand in line when they see those burly black arms. It's the truth. You'll have to fend them off with a stick. If I were a woman I'd be smitten. *(Pause.)*

STEPHEN: But you're not a woman.

WILDE: No. *(Beat.)* God, I'm *ravenous.* Let's go. *(Wilde dons his cape, they prepare to leave.)*

STEPHEN: I wish you hadn't read those pamphlets. They give a false impression.

WILDE: Don't be silly. Your people have great spirit. And in the face of tragic history.

STEPHEN: You can't wrap it up that easy sir. You don't know what it was like.

WILDE: *(Stops and looks at him.)* No. No I don't. But I'd be delighted to hear about it—*tomorrow.* Come along, where's your jacket?

STEPHEN: *(Getting his jacket.)* I just hope that buzzard reporter isn't behind us.

WILDE: We may find him ahead of us. He is a man as well. Come on, come on! *(Wilde exits, Stephen following.)*

THE SURVIVAL OF
THE SPECIES
Robert Shaffron

2 Men
  Ned (30s), a man whose wife is desperate to have a baby, and
  Glen (30s), his best friend.

Scene: Here and Now

Ned and Noreen have been trying to conceive for some time, and now
that Noreen is finally pregnant, exhausted Ned can finally relax. Ned
was never as enthusiastic about starting a family as his wife, and is
therefore numb when Glen, his friend, confesses to being the baby's
father.

О   О   О

(The bar. Glen and Ned, drunk.)
NED: I was watching one of those nature programs on viewer-sup-
    ported channel 13 last night. About salmon. Apparently, the
    birthrate among salmon has fallen off drastically. Salmon, it ap-
    pears, must return home, upstream, to spawn. Man-made
    dams, however, have been preventing them from swimming
    upstream, so they simply die off where they are without ever
    spawning. This has precipitated the creation of a good many
    hatcheries, where thousands and thousands of salmon babies
    are produced through the wonders of modern technology. It
    seems they scoop out all the roe from the girl salmons into a
    bucket, and then they pick up the males, tilt them over, and out
    gushes a most impressive stream of salmon semen into another
    bucket. And at the mere sight of this remarkably prolific flow of
    life-giving fluid, I began to cry. I actually wept. It was so... po-
    tent.
GLEN: That's very deep.
NED: It is.

GLEN: You're very deep.

NED: I am.

GLEN: You didn't used to be so deep. But now you are. Now you're deep.

NED: Why wasn't I deep before and now I am?

GLEN: Now you're tragic. Tragedy deepens a person.

NED: Tragic.

GLEN: A tragic figure.

NED: I don't think I'm tragic.

GLEN: Of course not. No one thinks of themselves as tragic. That's the beauty of tragedy.

NED: You mustn't tell Noreen.

GLEN: That you're tragic?

NED: That I'm sterile.

GLEN: No. I won't.

NED: I've thought it all out very carefully. The doctor confirmed that she's pregnant, right?

GLEN: Check.

NED: But I'm sterile, right?

GLEN: Check.

NED: So I never would have been able to get her pregnant anyway, right?

GLEN: Check.

NED: And all I've ever wanted is for Noreen to have what she wants, right?

GLEN: Check.

NED: So now Noreen has what she wants, which I wouldn't have been able to give her. And I have what I want, which is that she has what she wants, so what's a little transgression if it means we both have what we want?

GLEN: You're a very forgiving person.

NED: Yes. I am.

GLEN: That's an important quality.

NED: One can forgive almost anything to preserve a relationship, I think.

GLEN: You're right. Relationships are very important to preserve.

NED: Very important.

GLEN: We have a very deep relationship, you and I. We go way back. We've known each other longer than we've known our wives.

NED: Much longer.

GLEN: And I'm the only one who knows your secret.

NED: The only one.

GLEN: That's what friends do. Share each other's secrets.

NED: They do.

GLEN: And they forgive each other.

NED: Yes, they do.

GLEN: They forgive each other anything.

NED: Anything.

GLEN: No matter how disgusting it is.

NED: The more disgusting the better.

GLEN: And we're guys.

NED: Yes, we are.

GLEN: Guys do pretty disgusting things.

NED: That's the fun of being guys.

GLEN: But guys understand each other.

NED: Like brothers. Like a brotherhood of understanding…

GLEN: And forgiving…

NED: …And forgiving all the disgusting guy things we do.

GLEN: Ned.

NED: Glen.

GLEN: I'm glad you're glad Noreen's gonna have this baby.

NED: It's what she wants.

GLEN: Which is what you want.

NED: Which is what I want.

GLEN: And I'm glad I'm the only one you trusted with the secret that not even your wife knows.

NED: I'm glad, too.

GLEN: Ned.

NED: Glen.

GLEN: In the name of brotherhood, I want to share a secret with you that *my* wife doesn't know.

NED: If you're sure you want to.

GLEN: I'm sure.

NED: What.

GLEN: I'm the one that got Noreen pregnant… (*Pause.*)

NED: I see.

GLEN: Ned.

NED: You're the one.

GLEN: I'm the one.

NED: What you're saying. What you're telling me here is that you're. You're the father of my child.

GLEN: Yes.

NED: Well.

GLEN: You can hit me.

NED: Hit you.

GLEN: Yes. You can hit me. And then we can begin the process of reclaiming. Rebuilding our relationship. Then forgiveness can begin.

NED: Hit you. No.

GLEN: Please, Ned. You can.

NED: No. I can't. I don't want to.

GLEN: You don't want to. Of course you want to.

NED: No. I told you. No.

GLEN: Why not?

NED: Like you said. Forgiveness. I forgive you.

GLEN: Ned, do you understand what I'm saying? I got Noreen pregnant.

NED: I understand.

GLEN: I slept with your wife. I fucked your wife.

NED: Yes, Glen, I know how it works.

GLEN: Then hit me. I know you want to hit me. We're guys, right? That's what guys do.

NED: No. I explained it before. What you've done is, in effect, a favor. I couldn't get the job done. You did it for me.

GLEN: Ned. I've done a terrible thing. You must hit me. I deserve to be hit.

NED: That's all right. We can just pretend I've hit you, and move on from there.

GLEN: ARE YOU CRAZY? ARE YOU OUT OF YOUR FUCKING MIND?? WHAT KIND OF MAN ARE YOU?? YOU'RE NOT NOR- MAL!! I FUCKED YOUR WIFE!! NOW HIT ME, GODDAMNIT! I OUGHT TO BE PUNISHED!

NED: Glen.

GLEN: WHAT!?

NED: Hit yourself. (*Blackout.*)

THE TREATMENT
Martin Crimp

2 Men

Clifford (60s) an out-of-work playwright forced to sell his belongings on the street, and Simon (20s) a man who hates art.

Scene: New York City

As Simon, a disturbed man who keeps his wife tied to a chair in their apartment, looks through Clifford's things, the two men engage in a conversation that will ultimately reveal Simon's hatred and rage.

O   O   O

(An elderly man, Clifford, is selling dishes and other household goods arranged on a blanket. A young man, Simon, picks through the items. He's drinking from a bottle of beer inside a brown paper bag.)

CLIFFORD: I mapped out the course of my life very early on—in the fifties in fact. In the fifties I must've been your age, but already I had decided.

SIMON: How much is this?

CLIFFORD: (That one's ten.) I had decided that I would divide each year of my life into two halves. In one half of the year I would do whatever was necessary to live—usually as it turned out in the summer months—meatpacking on the tenth and fourteenth (of course I was stronger then) or maybe waiting tables.

SIMON: And this?

CLIFFORD: (Fifteen.) Last year for example I was security guard at the Museum of Modern Art because in recent years I've generally looked for something air-conditioned. And these modest jobs have given me the means.

SIMON: Fifteen for the *plate?*

CLIFFORD: To live because my outgoings are very low. That is Limoges. It belonged to my parents. It is not "a plate," it is Limoges. And then the rest of the year, *each* year (the forks and spoons are solid silver) each and every year what I've done—generally through the winter months, the fall and winter months—is I've risen early, often in the dark, and I've sat at my desk, which is mahogany and belonged to my father and which I would never sell even though it fills my room and I have to sleep curled up under it—I've sat at my father's desk—he lost everything in twenty-nine the year I was born—I've sat at that desk and every year without fail I have completed a play. That's forty-one shows in as many years. Now there's a word for that. The word my young friend is discipline.

SIMON: Discipline. Uh-huh. Is it?

CLIFFORD: As a young man I had a couple of big hits in the fifties. *(Simon smiles. He's not listening. He examines the silver.)* You don't believe me? In the fifties a couple of my shows were playing on Broadway. I have the programs right here. *(He pulls out some tattered programs.)* You see—big stars—*my* name. And when I say Broadway I mean uptown—proper theatres—not these holes that call themselves theatres where people who call themselves actors mouth the obscenities of people who call themselves writers. *(He chuckles.)* Two shows on Broadway. Then after that, nothing. *(He folds up the programs and puts them away.)*

SIMON: I like this fork.

CLIFFORD: Does that seem just to you? Is that justice?

SIMON: How much for the fork?

CLIFFORD: To dedicate your life to something, to an *art*.

SIMON: How much is the fork?

CLIFFORD: I'll take five for the fork. I send out scripts. Once in awhile I have a meeting with a young person like yourself who tells me my work is old-fashioned. I say to them that's also true of William Shakespeare. *(He chuckles.)*

SIMON: Uh-huh? You say five?

CLIFFORD: It's antique.

SIMON: I'll take it. *(He pays.)*

CLIFFORD: I can see you value things like this, beautiful things like this. *(Clifford pockets the five. He looks at Simon.)* It's unusual to find someone on the street who values things. Perhaps you know someone who... I mean could introduce me to someone who... Because I have *meetings* but I never—

SIMON: I have no interest in the theatre.

CLIFFORD: I see.

SIMON: I have no interest in any form of art.

CLIFFORD: Which is your right. I see that.

SIMON: I will not pay good money to be told that the world is a heap of shit.

CLIFFORD: Listen, I write comedies. I've no intention of—

SIMON: I won't sit in the dark to be told that it is an unweeded garden.

CLIFFORD: A garden.

SIMON: An unweeded (that's right) garden. Or that man is man's— Okay?—excrement. And these are men who have supposedly *thought* would you believe about the world, men who are respected, who have a place in *history*—

CLIFFORD: Our own excrement? Is that *Biblical?*

SIMON: But what I say to them *is,* the world is not a heap of shit, *you* my friend are the heap of shit... *(Nearby a car alarm goes off.)* ...the world is not a heap of shit because the sickness is *in here*...

CLIFFORD: In the brain. Okay. Listen—

SIMON: Right here—yes—in the brains of those individuals. People who practice so-called *art,* who urinate on their responsibility to others in order to burrow down into themselves, to drag up stories *out* of themselves.

CLIFFORD: You mean it's a chemical? Have you *studied* this?

SIMON: It could be a chemical, it could be an *experience* they've had. *(The alarm grows more piercing.)*

CLIFFORD: In the womb.

SIMON: Wherever.

CLIFFORD: (Because I believe that people *do have* experiences in the womb.)

SIMON: Wherever. It could be chemical. It could be their environment. But all I would say to them is get off my back. Get the fuck off of my back because I do not *need* that.

Permission Acknowledgments

THE APPRENTICE by Jack Gilhooley. Copyright © 1994, by Jack Gilhooley. Reprinted by per-misssion of the author. All inquiries should be directed to Jo Morello, Inc., 7342 Golfe Pointe Circle, Sarasota, FL 34243.

ARCADIA by Tom Stoppard. Copyright © 1993, by Tom Stoppard. Reprinted by permission of Faber & Faber, Inc. All inquiries should be directed to Faber & Faber, Inc, 50 Cross Street, Winchester, MA 01890.

ARTHUR & LEILA by Cherylene Lee. Copyright © 1993, by Cherylene Lee. Reprinted by permis-sion of the author. All inquiries should be directed to the author's agent, Bruce Ostler, Fifi Oscard Agency, Inc., 24 West 40th Street, New York, NY 10018.

BEFORE IT HITS HOME by Cheryl L. West. © Copyright 1993, by Cheryl L. West CAUTION: The reprinting of BEFORE IT HITS HOME by Cheryl L. West included in this volume is reprinted by permission of the author and Dramatists Play Service, Inc. The stage perfor-mance rights (other than first-class rights) are controlled exclusively by Dramatists Play Ser-vice, Inc., 440 Park Ave. South, New York, NY 10016. No professional or non-professional performance of the play (excluding first-class professional performance) may be given with-out obtaining in advance the written permission of Dramatists Play Service, Inc., and paying the requisite fee.

CANNED GOODS by Silas Jones. Copyright © 1994, by Silas Jones. Reprint by permission of the author. All inquiries concerning production or other rights to CANNED GOODS should be addressed in writing to the author's agent, Helen Merrill, Ltd., 435 West 23rd Street, Suite 1A New York, NY 10011, USA. No amateur or professional performance or reading of the play may be given without obtaining, in advance, the written permission of Helen Merrill, Ltd.

CARELESS LOVE by Len Jenkin. Copyright © 1993, by Len Jenkin. Reprinted by permission of the author. All inquiries should be directed to the author's agent, Scott Hudson, Writers and Artists Agency, 19 West 44th Street, Suite 1000, New York, NY 10036.

THE CAVALCADERS by Billy Roche. Copyright © 1994, by Billy Roche. Published by Nick Hern Books. All inquiries should be directed to Nick Hern Books, 14 Larden Road, London W3 7ST ENGLAND. Available in USA from Theatre Communications Corp.

THE CONFIRMATION by Kier Peters. Copyright © 1993, by Kier Peters. Reprinted by permis-sion of Sun & Moon Press, Los Angeles. All inquiries should be directed to Sun & Moon Press, 6026 Wilshire Blvd., Los Angeles, CA 90036.

COUP DE GRACE by Bill Ohanesian. Copyright © 1993, by Bill Ohanesian. Reprinted by per-mission of the author. All inquiries should be directed to B. Ohanesian, 1705 Neil Arm-strong Drive, #111, Montebello, CA 90640.

CUTE BOYS IN THEIR UNDERPANTS FIGHT THE EVIL TROLLS by Robert Coles. Copyright © 1994, by Robert Coles. Reprinted by permission of the author. All inquiries should be di-rected to Robert Coles, 80 Warren Street, #16, New York, NY 10007.

THE DARKER FACE OF THE EARTH A verse play by Rita Dove. Book publication by Story Line Press, Brownsville, Oregon, 1994. Copyright © 1994, by Rita Dove. Reprinted by permis-sion of the author. All inquiries should be directed to Rita Dove, Dept. of English, University of Virginia, Charlottesville, VA 22903.

THE ENDS OF THE EARTH by Morris Panych. Copyright © 1993, by Morris Panych. Reprinted with permission from Morris Panych, Talon Books, Ltd., Vancouver Canada. All inquiries should be directed to Patricia Ney, Christopher Banks & Associates, Inc., 6 Adelaide Street East, Suite 610, Toronto, Ontario M5C 1H6 Canada.

THE FAMILY OF MANN by Theresa Rebeck. Copyright © 1994, by Theresa Rebeck. All rights reserved. CAUTION: Professionals and amateurs are hereby warned that THE FAMILY OF MANN by Theresa Rebeck is subject to a royalty. It is fully protected under the copyright laws of the United States of America, and of all countries covered by the International Copyright Union (including the Dominion of Canada and the rest of the British Common-